The Complete
House Rabbit

Carolina James

Printed in China through Printworks Int. Ltd.

contents

Dedication
This book is dedicated to all bunnies at rescue centres and those
who deserve better.
Also to Carolina, Benjamin and Sweetpea with all my love.

chapter 1

Why Indoor Rabbits?

Rabbits can live happily indoors, just like a cat or dog. They are wonderful companions, quiet, clean and easy to litter-train. They are no more destructive than other household pets if you take some basic precautions and give them a variety of toys.

Traditionally, rabbits have been kept in hutches in the garden but outdoor bunnies are likely to become neglected once the novelty wears off and the weather gets cold. Single rabbits, in particular, end up living a very sad existence confined in a hutch without a companion. Often, garden rabbits get very little exercise or are left unsupervised in the garden where, eventually, they escape or fall prey to dogs, foxes, large birds and other predators. Not many people realise that even in a sturdy hutch or run, a rabbit can become very stressed or even die of a heart attack when she sees or smells a predator.

Rabbits love to explore.

If you keep your rabbit outdoors, you will have to water, feed and keep her company whatever the weather. Bringing the rabbit into your home makes it easier to meet her social and physical needs and gives you a chance to really get to know and bond with your rabbit.

Rabbits are lively and active in the mornings and evenings so make ideal companions for working people. House rabbits get more company and attention from people and become family pets as opposed to children's pets. They also have the chance to exercise in one or more bunny-proofed rooms without the fear of being teased or chased and attacked by predators.

The idea of keeping rabbits indoors may seem unusual to some people, but it wasn't so long ago that dogs and cats were also kept outside. An outdoor rabbit will adapt quickly and easily to being a house rabbit. All you have to do is prepare a suitable living/running space.

If you have a garden, your house rabbit can have the best of both worlds and exercise outside when you have time to supervise her. Always move your rabbit back in after dark, during bad weather and whenever you have to go out.

Carolina enjoying a leisurely breakfast.

Time for tea; I'll just help myself!

5

If you don't have a garden, you can bring the outside world in by giving your rabbit a digging box full of hay, straw, peat, soil, sand or other material. Grass, weeds and other plants are easily grown in pots and windowboxes. Indoor bunnies also enjoy looking outside by sitting on window seats, or you can build a ramp to allow your rabbit to hop to the window and enjoy the view.

If you cannot keep your rabbit indoors (for example if you are allergic or the landlord forbids it) I recommend you keep your bunny in a shed, disused garage or other outdoor building to protect her from predators and weather extremes, especially during the night.

Your rabbit must have some form of shade and protection whilst outside, for example a ramp or wooden tunnel.

chapter 2

Are You The Right Type Of Person?

A wicker basket is a fun place for your rabbit to hide under.

Caring for a rabbit is a great responsibility and extends to the whole of the animal's life (7-10 years, and up to 14 in some cases). You may be surprised to know that rabbits are not inexpensive, low-maintenance pets and can almost be as much work as having a dog (or a toddler). The following points will help you decide if a bunny is right for you:

- Are you willing to devote at least an hour a day to your rabbit?
- If you have children, are you willing to supervise them when they are with the rabbit, and be responsible for her welfare yourself?
- Can you afford to buy a large cage/pen, food, bedding, litter and so on?
- Can you provide shelter for your rabbit overnight, for example in a shed, garage, or in the house?
- Can you provide an escape-proof run or garden for daytime exercise (under supervision)?

- Can you provide a companion for your rabbit, for example a guinea pig or another rabbit, or can you keep your rabbit company for a few hours a day?
- Are you willing to get to know your rabbit at floor level?
- Can you afford to have your rabbit vaccinated twice a year and neutered?
- Can you afford to pay for veterinary treatment when your rabbit is ill? (This could add up to several hundred pounds or more in your rabbit's lifetime.)
- Do you have at least 1 or 2 rooms where you don't smoke, where the tv/hi-fi are not on constantly and where there are no expensive carpets, pieces of furniture, and wallpaper to worry about?
- Are you willing to make some compromises in your furniture arrangements?
- Are you willing to follow safety guidelines?
- Are you willing to do more cleaning than you would do without a rabbit?
- Are you willing to clean up litter-training accidents?
- Can you afford to board your rabbit or do you know someone who can look after her and exercise her when you go on holiday?
- Will you take your rabbit with you if you move?

Widget enjoying a cuddle with her foster mummy.

Living with a house rabbit can be a wonderful experience for some people. However, before you bring your bunny indoors make sure you have all the information and everyone in your family shares your desire for a house rabbit.

Rabbits and Children

Contrary to common stereotype, rabbits are not very suitable for children under 10 years of age. The liveliness and noisiness of small children can be stressful for a sensitive and timid creature like the rabbit. Children will want to pick up the rabbit and carry her like a soft toy, while rabbits are ground-loving creatures who prefer to be petted at floor level. If a rabbit is chased or held against her will she may kick and bite to defend herself. It is estimated that most children lose interest within a month of having a bunny. So, unless the parents are willing to consider the rabbit their pet, and take full responsibility for her care, it is kinder not to adopt her in the first place.

It is unreasonable to expect a child of any age to take on responsibility for a rabbit. What normally happens is that after a short time the novelty wears off and the rabbit becomes neglected or mistreated. Forcing a child to continue caring for his rabbit will just make the rabbit a source of frustration. Children learn mainly by example; so, if the adults in the family are not interested in the rabbit and see her as a chore, the children will soon follow suit. In addition children's interests change as they get older, so a 9 year old child who is very fond of her rabbit may be more interested in boyfriends and parties a couple of years later. Rabbits are long-lived animals and deserve to be treated with love and care for the whole of their lives. This is unlikely to happen if the rabbit is solely the child's pet.

Naturally we don't want to stop families with children from adopting a rabbit but care should be taken when mixing rabbits with small children. Do not leave small children and the

Snoopy prefers to be petted while he is on the floor.

rabbit together unsupervised. If the children are too noisy and chase or frighten the rabbit, they should be kept in separate rooms whenever possible. Provide several hiding places which are easy for the rabbit to reach but not the children - behind the sofa, under a bed, a box or pen with the entrance facing a wall with a gap big enough for the bunny to hop in and out. Show your children how to pet the rabbit on her forehead, behind her ears and on the upper back. Teach them to stop when the rabbit looks frightened or has had enough of being cuddled. Children can also befriend a rabbit by brushing her and giving her food, either from a dish or the palm of the hand (not between the fingers). We do not recommend letting children pick up their rabbit, especially if she does not like being held, for their own safety as well as the bunny's.

chapter 3

Bunny-Proofing

The kitchen may be a good place to keep a house bunny like Benjamin.

Rabbit-proofing your home, preferably before you introduce your rabbit, is essential to limit damage to your property and protect your bunny from harm. In the beginning I recommend you keep your rabbit in an easily proofed room where you spend a lot of time, for example the kitchen or living room. Choosing a suitable room will reduce the amount of bunny-proofing needed; naturally it is best to avoid rooms with carpet, wallpaper, expensive items or a lot of telephone/electric cables.

As a general rule, objects within 60cm of the floor are at risk from bunny attacks and should be protected or removed. Young rabbits in particular can be very active and inquisitive so you'll need to be extra vigilant during exercise times. Remember that a bored rabbit or one who is left alone for most of the time is more likely to create jumping, digging and chewing diversions with your furniture and home decor. For this reason it's important to combine bunny-proofing with toys, as described in Chapter 5. It is also a good idea to decide in advance whether some rooms are to be no-go areas to your rabbit.

Rabbit-proofing may appear laborious but most of what's required is a one-off job. Once an area is bunny-proofed, all you have to do is check from time to time that the rabbit hasn't damaged or removed protective covers.

Safeguarding your home

- Valuable books and documents should be moved out of reach if your rabbit enjoys chewing them. Some rabbits seem to gravitate around the latest copy of your favourite magazine or TV programmes. Paper-trained bunnies may leave liquid and solid calling cards on anything made of paper left lying on the floor.
- Avoid leaving handbags, shoes and clothes on the floor or low furniture.
- Rabbits tend to dig at the end of tunnels (behind the sofa, between a piece of furniture and the wall and so on). Put a straw mat or a piece of carpet at the end of the tunnel and hold it down with furniture on either side. Alternatively, leave an old Yellow Pages or a tub filled with paper, hay, straw and towels for your rabbit to dig in.
- Neutering or spaying your bunny will help to reduce destructiveness. You should also keep her toenails clipped. Swallowing carpet can be dangerous for your rabbit so follow up excessive carpet-chewing with a petroleum laxative from your pet supply shop.

Plenty of toys plus a tunnel for exploring and resting in should keep Poppy amused.

- If your rabbit loves gnawing on wooden furniture, offer her plenty of chew toys (such as untreated pine blocks, apple tree branches, seagrass mats or cardboard boxes). Avoid putting litter-trays near light-coloured walls and furniture to prevent urine-staining.
- Upholstered beds and sofas that are raised off the floor are very attractive to rabbits and some will build a nest in the soft padding. A cardboard box or wooden frame lower than the base of the bed or sofa should keep your rabbit away.

Jeanine resting after a play session.

Alternatively, offer her a box with shredded paper, straw and old towels for digging. If your rabbit likes chewing holes in the back of the settee, give her a closed cardboard box full of straw, paper or fabric. Make a small gap in one of the sides to encourage your rabbit to chew her way in.

- Prevent access to a dangerous or non rabbit-proofed area by using furniture and other objects (cardboard boxes, straw baskets and so on) as blocking devices. Hi-fi speakers can be positioned to deter your bunny from hopping behind the hi-fi and chewing the cables. Use phone books or flat cardboard boxes to prevent access to the back of the cooker, fridge or washing machine.

- Baby gates and puppy pen panels can be used to confine a bunny to a room or part of it while still making her feel part of the family. You can use a similar gate to stop your rabbit from going in the garden if you can't supervise her. Baby gates are also useful for preventing a rabbit from hopping up or downstairs.

- Don't leave your remote or cordless telephone lying around or your bunny might chew the soft buttons. Rabbits find telephone, aerial and electric cables irresistible. Chewing them may result in the rabbit (or another pet or person) being burned or electrocuted, so it is essential to conceal all wiring that is within her reach. Don't rely solely on supervision or training to prevent damage to your cables - a bunny can gnaw through them in an instant as soon as your back is turned. The first step is to gather and conceal excess cable wherever possible (for example under a mattress or behind some furniture). Protect your wiring with clear plastic water piping from a DIY shop. Cut along its length with a Stanley knife and wrap around the cable. Water piping is sold by the foot and comes in various diameters. Some rabbits will still nibble on the tubing but this gives you enough time to replace it or use a stronger type of cable cover. I suggest you secure the piping with sticky tape near a plug, switch or adaptor to prevent slipping.

- In addition to cables, rabbits enjoy nibbling on articles made of rubber or soft plastic (such as garden hosepipes, shoes, inflatable sun beds and foam cushions). Keep such items out of reach whenever possible.
- Chairs should be pushed all the way under tables to prevent an energetic bunny from jumping on the desktop.
- Anti-chew repellents for kittens and puppies can be sprayed on furniture and carpets as a deterrent. Spray daily until your rabbit has lost interest in the forbidden item. Other odours a bunny may find repellent include aftershave, perfume, deodorant and so on. Some people have tried using red pepper sauce or bitter apple to stop their bunny from gnawing but it is better to put her off with an unpleasant smell before she actually nibbles on something.

Rabbits love boxes and shady places.

- If your rabbit likes stripping the wallpaper, cover lower wall areas with flat cardboard or plexiglas. Offer her plenty of things to shred, such as old magazines and telephone books.
- Protect skirting boards and other furniture by nailing a thin strip of untreated pine on them. Combine this method with chew toys and with training your rabbit not to gnaw on these items.

Keeping your rabbit safe

- Doors leading to non bunny-proofed rooms should be kept closed at all times. Open and close doors gently to prevent your rabbit from getting caught. Drafts may suddenly slam a door shut, so use a door wedge when you air the rooms. Slamming a door or bursting into a room will also frighten your rabbit. Under no circumstances leave your front door open or ajar because it only takes a few seconds for your bunny to escape.
- As your bunny starts following you around the house, take care not to step on her or kick her accidentally. Get into the habit of looking before you walk and preferably wear soft shoes or slippers when you are at home.
- If your rabbit spends a lot of time in the kitchen, she may run between your feet while you're cooking or using knives, scissors and so on. Take extra care when

handling hot food and liquids. If possible, use the rings at the back of the cooker so if a liquid boils over it will not burn your rabbit.

- Rabbits can slip on smooth floors and they can catch cold on some linoleum/stone floors. Avoid this by giving your bunny something to rest on, for example grass mats, towels, cotton or synthetic sheepskin rugs, or a dog basket.
- Be careful not to drop anything on your rabbit, especially hot drinks, food, sharp or heavy items. Avoid piling things high (such as magazines, books or dishes) in case they fall on top of your rabbit.
- Keep all medicines out of reach.
- Pick up small objects that can be swallowed by the rabbit, including rubber bands, drawing pins, needles, paper clips, jewellery and so on.
- Many indoor plants are toxic, so move them to a high shelf or cabinet top where the bunny can't reach them.
- Friends and visitors are probably not used to having a house rabbit around, so should be reminded to be vigilant.

Spok and Ayosha, two happy and contented rabbits.

chapter 4

Accommodation

A large pen is a good way to introduce your house bunny to living indoors.

Baby rabbits are good climbers and can get into all sorts of scrapes.

Ideally, an indoor rabbit should have the run of the house - or at least part of it - 24 hours a day. If she needs to be confined, you can simply keep her in a bunny-proofed room and close the door as you would do with a cat or dog. Over the years I have kept my own rabbits as well as all my foster rabbits in this way. However, if this is your first house rabbit, and she is very young or destructive, you may wish to get a large puppy pen and gradually increase her running time rather than starting without a pen and having to confine her later. This will help to train your rabbit and will give you time to do some extra bunny-proofing if necessary.

The puppy pen should be large and

15

A varnished floor is virtually indestructible and is easy to clean.

comfortable - at least 4-6 times the size of the bunny when fully stretched. Allow room for food dishes, litter tray and toys on top of that. If you are getting a baby rabbit, bear in mind how big she will grow. The pen should also be tall enough to allow your rabbit to stand on her back feet. However large the pen is, it isn't a replacement for free-running time. A rabbit should have the chance to hop around one or more rooms (or a safe run in the garden) for at least 5 hours a day.

Ceramic food bowls are difficult to tip over and cannot be chewed.

When your rabbit is better trained and your home (or the rooms she will have access to) has been thoroughly rabbit-proofed, you can let her hop around even when you are not there. A rabbit with lots of room to hop around in behaves in a more natural and varied way than a caged bunny.

Being crepuscular, rabbits tend to sleep during the day and night, becoming active first thing in the morning and the evening. Be certain you let your rabbit exercise before you leave for work and when you return home in the evenings.

Even when a rabbit has plenty of space to move around, she may still get bored, especially if she's on her own. A bored rabbit is more likely to be destructive if it helps to pass the time. To prevent this it is necessary to supply her with lots of interesting items. I have found the following items to be very popular: cardboard boxes, baskets, wooden tunnels, twigs, digging boxes, magazines, phone books, grass mats and so on (see Chapter 5). If you are out of the house for long periods you should consider getting your rabbit a companion.

Pen/Cage features and furnishings

- Doors: Cages should have a side/front-opening door for the bunny to go in and out and a top-opening door big enough to put in the litter tray. The top door is also useful for picking up the rabbit since approaching from above is less threatening to her. If you have a wire cage you may be able to enlarge existing doors. As your pet becomes litter-trained and less destructive you can leave the cage door open for her all the time.

- Wire floors: Wire floors are not suitable for rabbits because they don't have padded feet like dogs and cats. If you must get a cage or pen with a wire bottom, you should provide your rabbit with a cardboard/wooden board or a blanket/rug/towel to rest on otherwise she will either spend all her time in the litter tray or she may develop sore hocks. A solid floor (plastic or wooden) is more comfortable than a wire one.

- Water bottle/bowl: Water kept in a bowl offers a more natural way of drinking but tends to get dirty and can be spilt easily. You can provide water in a bottle with a double-ball valve to avoid constant dripping. Change the water daily and wash the bottle in soapy water, rinsing thoroughly. Place the bottle out of direct sunlight so the water stays cool. From time to time it's a good idea to check the metal tube to make sure it is not blocked. Rabbits normally get used to drinking from a bottle very quickly but, if your rabbit doesn't get the idea, you need to show her gently and provide a bowl just in case. Use a heavy earthenware pot that the bunny cannot tip over easily. Fresh clean water should always be available.

- Food dish: The best type of food dish is a heavy clay or ceramic pot with wide or sloping sides (available from your pet supply store). Lightweight plastic bowls tend to be nibbled at, particularly if the rabbit is bored, and can easily be gripped in the bunny's teeth and overturned. Avoid using designer pottery for your rabbit as it may contain lead.

- Hay rack: We put hay and straw in the litter trays/digging boxes and change it at least once a day. If you use a different type of litter, you may wish to buy a hay rack so the hay/straw remains clean. This can be hooked to the side of the pen or the edge of the litter tray. Or, leave a handful of hay and straw in your rabbit's bed or litter tray.

- Litter tray: Depending on the rabbit and the size of the cage, put one or two litter trays in the back corners. Once your rabbit gets used to urinating in her tray, it will be easier to litter-train her around the house.

  If your rabbit enjoys turning over the litter tray, you may need to clamp it to the side of the cage or drill two small holes and tie it to the wire mesh.

Sheltered corner

Rabbits usually like to have a covered area to retreat to when they want some peace and quiet. A cardboard or wooden box with 2 doors or a wooden tunnel is ideal for this purpose. Alternatively, you can drape a towel or blanket over one side of the pen. Putting the pen under a table will give the bunny some privacy as well as protect her from bright lights overhead.

A rabbit should regard her pen as her home, a safe haven where she can eat, do her business, play and sleep in peace. Respecting your rabbit's territory will also help when it comes to litter-training as the bunny

Boxes can be converted into rabbit dens.

will hopefully mark her pen and avoid urinating and depositing pellets all around the house.

To reinforce this we recommend you:

- Place the food dish/water bottle at the front of the cage so you can refill them with minimum interference.
- Wait until the bunny is in her running space before cleaning the cage or emptying the litter tray.
- Avoid pushing or picking up your rabbit from her home unless you really have to. Simply open the door and coax her out with her favourite food. If the cage is on legs, build a ramp or steps so the bunny can come and go as she pleases. You can also train her to hop directly in her travel cage, for example if you need to carry her to the outside run, by using a treat.
- Don't put your rabbit back in her cage, then slam the door closed or you will make this look like punishment. Shepherd her in gently and, as soon as she pops in, give her a treat and lots of praise. Wait a few seconds before closing the door slowly.

- Avoid putting your hand in the cage or interfering with your bunny's property unnecessarily.
- Don't do anything unpleasant to your bunny while she's in her home.

Building a cage

You can build a cage with a board of 12mm plywood and 0.5 inch or 1 inch square welded mesh which the rabbits can't nibble at. Since it's an indoor cage, there is no need to have solid walls and you can use mesh on all sides and the roof. Avoid using paint or wood preservative within the cage or limit these to the floor and buy a non-toxic variety. Washable vinyl flooring is ideal to lay on the wooden base (remove if bunny chews on it). The minimum recommended cage size for one small to medium size rabbit is 4ft x 2ft x 2ft (1.2m x 61cm x 61cm) and, for two small to medium size rabbits, 5ft x 2ft x 2ft (1.5m x 61cm x 61cm). The bigger the better, and the happier the rabbit will be.

The cage must be large enough for toys, food bowls and litter trays.

Two-storey cages with a ramp or steps between the floors are very popular with rabbits and take up less room than a large single-tier pen. Alternatively, if the cage is very tall, you can put a shelf along the back wall so the bunny can hop up and down and use it as a resting platform or look-out point.

Types of accommodation

Even if you intend to build a very large pen later, it is often convenient to start with a cage from your pet supply shop and replace it later.

You can build a cage with plywood and wire mesh as described above or buy a large puppy pen from a pet supply store. Puppy pens tend to be taller than rabbit cages but have a shallow tray and sometimes a wire floor or no floor at all (cover the

Plastic dog beds are also appreciated by house bunnies.

Snowy demonstrating that your rabbit may adopt any object that he can hop into!

bottom with a soft rug or vinyl flooring as described above). A child's playpen also makes a good indoor cage although it doesn't have a side door for bunny's use.

Many rabbits like to sleep in a plastic dog bed lined with a synthetic sheepskin rug. The high sides give a bunny a feeling of security and protect her from drafts at floor level. If the dog bed is extra large you can even put a litter tray in one corner as you would in a cage. Place the dog bed under a table or in a quiet spot where the bunny won't be disturbed. Furnish it with a rug/blanket/towel, toys, a handful of hay and straw, food dishes and mineral/salt licks. Dog beds combine high sides with easy access and are ideal for elderly and infirm rabbits.

If you don't have a cage your bunny will need a cosy area to call her own, perhaps under a table or in a recess fenced off with puppy pen panels or a baby gate. Furnish it with your rabbit's favourite toys, bed, rug, food/water bowl and, of course, litter tray. A burrow-like space - for example, a cardboard box with two entrances - will be a welcome addition. As with a pen, try to do the cleaning-up while the bunny is not in residence. Never annoy the bunny when she is in her home.

Position

The rabbit's cage or bed should be:

- in a room where you spend a lot of time - for example, the kitchen, living room, bedroom, study and so on.
- in a fairly quiet area. Rabbits become anxious when they hear loud noises such as a blaring tv/hi-fi system, doors slamming, noisy birds/dogs or children screaming.
- in a bright spot but not near a sunny window or strong artificial lights.
- in a well ventilated room but away from draughts.
- away from radiators, fireplaces, cookers, and other sources of heat.
- away from unpleasant and strong smells such as disinfectant, cigarette smoke, strong cleaning agents and carburettor cleaner.

In a home with young children I recommend putting the pen with the entrance door facing a wall or a piece of furniture, with a gap big enough for the bunny to pop in and out, but not for the children. Or place the bunny's dog bed/cardboard box in a hard-to-reach place, for instance under a bed or behind the sofa.

If you can't keep your bunny indoors at night, set up her cage in a shed, disused garage or other outdoor building. A conservatory is also fine if it is airy and has blinds to keep the summer sun out; do keep a watchful eye on the temperature though. Leaving the bunny in a hutch in the garden is not recommended because cats, foxes and other predators will probably come and visit your rabbit.

If your rabbit is in a shed, be certain you leave the windows open on warm days and fit a welded mesh panel to keep predators out. You can fit a similar panel to the door frame if need be. Secure all windows and doors at night.

Balcony/terrace

If you have a balcony or terrace you could make this into a bunny exercise area. Get your rabbit used to outdoor temperatures gradually if she has never been outside. You will need to tie some welded mesh along the railings (minimum 1 metre high). Cover the gap under the railings with some wooden boards which exclude drafts and are also good for nibbling.

Make sure cats cannot jump into the balcony and harm your pet. If the floor is cold or slippery give your bunny some straw mats and a plastic dog bed to sit on. An awning or beach umbrella will shelter your rabbit from rain and strong sunlight. You can also drape a towel over a chair to provide some shade. Do not leave the chair near the balustrade or your bunny could jump over it. Keep an eye out for predatory birds and never leave your rabbit on the balcony unsupervised.

If you don't have a garden you can grow grass and other plants on your balcony (in pots, troughs and so on). A storage box or large tray full of peat, sand or garden compost is a good place for rolling, digging and urinating.

Keep poisonous plants out of your rabbit's reach.

Rabbits in the garden should always be supervised.

Making the garden safe for your rabbit

Many house rabbits have the run of the garden as well as the house. Rabbits like hopping around the garden, jumping, digging and sniffing the air. They may spend several hours a day nibbling at the grass and plants and sleeping under a bush or behind some pots.

You should get your rabbit used to outdoor temperatures gradually. Don't let your rabbit out in very cold, windy or wet weather. Many rabbits like playing in the snow in winter. This is fine as long as your bunny stays active and you don't leave her unattended in extreme cold.

If your rabbit has never been outside, take care she doesn't eat too much grass or plants in the beginning (especially if they're wet). Your rabbit may find new sounds frightening, for example the noise of traffic, helicopters, lawnmowers, noisy birds and other animals, so stay near your bunny and be ready to reassure her.

Before you let your rabbit go outside it's essential to make the garden escape-proof. You can do this by using rolls of wire mesh (minimum 3ft or 1 metre high) with wooden posts or bamboo canes as a support. If possible, buy some wire netting 5ft (1.5 metres) high and bury it 16 inches (40cm) or more into the ground so that your rabbit cannot dig her way out of the garden.

Your garden shouldn't be so big or full of plants that if your bunny hides you cannot find her. You should be able to see all parts of it from the house; check on your bunny frequently to make sure she is safe. If your garden is very big and you can only see a limited area from the house, it is better to put your bunny in a large run or enclosure.

Food and water are still necessary when your rabbit is in his pen.

Take care not to use weedkillers and other chemicals around the garden. Find out about poisonous plants and discard them or keep them away from your pet.

Some people say that rabbits can sense which plants are good for them and which aren't, but this is not always the case. One of my rabbits would eat box and privet if given the chance and they are both poisonous! Other plants like herbs are not toxic but will give your rabbit an upset tummy if eaten in large quantities, so grow them on windowsills or keep them on a stand or table where your rabbit cannot reach them.

You must supervise your bunny at all times when she is outside. Birds of prey could swoop down and attack your rabbit while you are not looking. Neighbours' cats and dogs may jump into the garden and harm your rabbit. Look out for squirrels, foxes and other wild animals. If your bunny is frightened by a predator she may injure herself trying to get away or die of shock before she's even caught.

You can make an enclosure using bamboo canes and a roll of wire netting as described above (minimum 33ft or 10 metre long). Make sure your rabbit can't escape by digging and lifting the wire mesh with her muzzle or leaping over the fence (some rabbits can easily jump 3ft or 90cm high). It is better to buy welded mesh rather than chicken wire so your rabbit cannot nibble through it. Check the fence regularly - in our garden it is pushed up by a squirrel almost daily. This type of enclosure is flexible and can be moved to a different part of the garden from time to time. It can also be rolled up and put away when it's not needed but it doesn't have a gate. To go in you will need to push the wire mesh down or use two garden chairs as steps.

You can build an enclosure with a gate by joining several panels made of welded mesh stretched across a wooden frame. If you are planning to build a permanent enclosure, bury the wire netting at least 16 inches (40cm) into the ground or ask a builder to make a concrete sill to stop your bunny from digging under the fence.

A safer way to give your rabbit exercise is to build a run with welded mesh stretched over a wooden frame. The run should be at least 4ft x 10ft x 2ft 6ins (1.2m x 3m x 75cm) high (depending on the size of your rabbit). It should have a solid plywood area at one end (to shelter your rabbit from predators, bad weather and direct sunlight) and a hinged or removable roof so you can pick up your rabbit. It is best to peg the run to the ground to stop winds from tipping it over and prevent dogs and other animals from getting in. If you want to add a wire floor for safety, give your rabbit a thick layer of clean hay/straw for resting on, digging and nibbling. Your rabbit will still be able to eat some grass through the gaps in the mesh. Don't forget to hook her water bottle to one of the side panels.

Moving the run to a new area at frequent intervals will provide fresh grazing.

Set up the run or enclosure in a sheltered area away from strong winds and direct sunlight (under a tree would be ideal). If your garden is very sunny you can put the run under a beach umbrella or build a plywood roof. Move the run every day or two to give your rabbit a fresh grazing patch and a new part of the garden to explore.

Getting your rabbit to go indoors

If your bunny has the run of the garden, she might not want to return indoors in the

evenings or when you go out. One way of getting your rabbit to go into the house is to train her to come when called (or when you rattle the peanut tin).

You can also teach your rabbit the "Home" command. Simply walk (not run) behind your rabbit saying "Home, X" (where X is her name). Your bunny will soon learn she has to go indoors. When she does, give her a food reward, praise and a cuddle.

Picking up a rabbit from the enclosure

It can be hard to catch a rabbit when she is in a large run or enclosure. Try not to frighten her by chasing and grabbing her.

A gentle but determined approach may be necessary when it is time to catch your rabbit.

Slowly walk behind your rabbit and get her into a corner (if your bunny keeps running up and down this may take a few minutes). You can use two hinged panels to trap her gently against the side of the run. The rabbit will know when she can't escape and will let you pick her up. If she doesn't like to be handled, get her to hop into a travel cage and carry her indoors in this way.

There are many ways of making the garden or enclosure into a more interesting place for your rabbit. You could provide:

A waterproof wooden tunnel in use.

- One or two crates for climbing on or hiding in. Check that there aren't any nails or staples sticking out.
- An upside-down wooden tub for jumping on.
- A clay pipe for running in and out.
- Wooden tunnels and boxes as described earlier, but made of waterproof plywood.
- A wooden step for climbing on and resting under.
- A big log or tree stump for hopping up and down.
- A willow or apple tree branch for your rabbit to nibble at; make sure it is from a healthy tree which hasn't been sprayed with insecticides and other chemicals.
- Stones, twigs (such as hazelnut or apple twigs), one or two bricks and some leaves for added interest.
- A peat or compost heap for your rabbit to dig and roll in.
- A heap of straw for digging and nibbling.
- A few potted plants - leave some space between the pots to create little alleyways for your rabbit. If you plant a small tree or long-stemmed plant in a big pot your bunny will be able to climb on the pot as well (protect the stem of the plant if necessary).
- An inflatable sunbed for jumping up and down and sleeping on (remove if bunny nibbles at it).
- One or two garden chairs and a low plastic table for climbing on and sleeping under. Draping a towel or an old sheet

Rabbits will check most things to see if they are edible.

L to r: Sweetpea helping in the garden. Ayosha choosing to sit on the chair, not under it. Note the use of draped towels to provide shade and privacy.

over them will prevent your bunny from slipping and make the area underneath sheltered and cosy. In the summer it will also create a shady spot for your rabbit.

- You could also plant sunflowers, marigolds, carrots and parsley inside the enclosure. Take care to avoid those vegetables and herbs which will give your rabbit an upset stomach if eaten in large quantities.

Carrots are a firm favourite with Spok, Ayosha and Snowy.

chapter 5

Diet and Exercise

Disabled bunny Ginger having her breakfast.

Grass is an essential part of your bunny's diet.

A rabbit's diet should consist of rabbit mix, good quality hay, fresh vegetables and water. Anything in addition to that is considered a treat and should be fed in limited amounts. Dried food should be fresh, high in fibre (minimum 13%, but higher is better), with a protein content of 10-14% for adult rabbits and around 16% for baby rabbits. Make sure your rabbit eats every part of the mix, and doesn't just pick out the tasty bits, or she will not be getting a balanced diet. This may result in serious health problems later on, such as dental and skeletal problems. Rabbit food should be stored in an airtight container in a cool, dry place.

Grass/meadow hay is essential to a healthy digestive system, reducing the risk of hairballs and other blockages and helping the bunny produce dry, odour-free pellets. Other good sources of fibre are straw and apple twigs. Fresh hay and straw should be available 24 hours a day. Keep it in a bag with a few holes for ventilation in a cool, dry spot.

Rabbits should be given a variety of fresh foods every day (at least 3 or 4 different types). Choose both dark leafy greens and root vegetables, and try different ones from time to time. Avoid rhubarb, beans, corn and potato peelings, and feed spinach and kale for no

Sweetpea enjoying a selection of fresh fruit and vegetables.

Carolina tipping over a lightweight food bowl.

Some of the author's foster rabbits sharing a meal of rabbit mix.

more than a few days at a time. Carrot and fruit such as apple, pear, banana, melon and grapes are high in sugar and should only be given in small quantities. Wash and dry all fresh food thoroughly before feeding it to your bunny. Never give vegetables straight from the fridge because cold, wet vegetables can cause bloat.

Rabbits enjoy nibbling on grass and garden weeds like plantain, dandelion, clover, chickweed, goosegrass and shepherd's purse. Grass can also be grown in pots or trays if you don't have a garden. Don't let your rabbit eat grass clippings or wet grass because they can cause severe digestive problems. Rabbits should always have access to fresh, clean water in a bowl or drinking bottle.

Rabbits up to 7 months old should have free access to rabbit mix and meadow/alfalfa hay. From 3 months old, offer small quantities of fresh foods introduced one at a time. Increase amounts gradually. If a certain vegetable doesn't agree with your rabbit, simply remove it from the diet.

Rabbits over 8 months old should be fed about one third of a cup of dried food per 2.75kg (6lb) body weight. If you started with junior rabbit mix, change slowly to lower protein adult food. Gradually remove alfalfa and increase grass hay. Slowly increase fresh foods to about 2 cups of vegetables and 1or 2 tablespoons of fruit per 2.75kg (6lb) body weight.

With elderly rabbits (over 6 years old), continue the normal diet if the weight is stable. Weak, older rabbits may need more dried food to keep their weight up. Alfalfa hay can be given to underweight rabbits, provided calcium levels are normal. Yearly blood tests are recommended for senior rabbits.

Dr Susan Brown's Hay and Vegetable Diet

Overweight rabbits and those who produce smelly, unformed droppings usually do better without any dried food. Slowly reduce the amount of rabbit mix and increase the vegetables over a period of several weeks. Make sure the rabbit eats a variety of fresh foods and at least one vegetable a day which contains vitamin A (parsley, broccoli, beetroot greens, collard greens, edible pea pods, watercress, carrot and carrot tops). Encourage the rabbit to eat more hay and straw by providing fresh handfuls two or three times a day. Offer your bunny apple twigs to chew on and a vitamin/mineral block.

Sometimes you may see your rabbit eat her own droppings directly from the anus. These caecal pellets are softer, shinier and have a stronger smell than the normal hard and round faeces. They usually come in clusters and are rich in vitamins and proteins that your rabbit needs to stay healthy. Although ingesting droppings may appear distasteful to us, it is normal and necessary for your rabbit.

Occasionally a rabbit will pass these droppings with the dry pellets instead of eating them. This is not considered diarrhoea and, if it only happens from time to time, is not a cause for concern. However if the rabbit leaves a lot of caecal pellets uneaten, or produces messy droppings (usually caecal pellets mixed with the normal faeces), it means her diet is too rich in protein and doesn't contain enough fibre. Please refer to the feeding guidelines above.

Clementine and Spok inspect the greens.

Exercise

Rabbits need plenty of exercise, just like dogs and cats. A bunny who gets the chance to hop around is happy, busy and interested in her surroundings. Regular exercise also benefits the heart, lungs, muscle and bone structure and keeps your bunny healthy.

Even free-range bunnies can get bored sometimes, particularly single bunnies. An animal friend will encourage your rabbit to exercise more and keep her company when you are not at home. You can also provide toys and furniture to keep your bunny occupied (see overleaf for some ideas).

House rabbits should not be kept singly, if at all possible.

All sorts of articles may used as toys.

It is always a good idea to give your rabbit something interesting to do, particularly if you only have one rabbit and if she is on her own for several hours a day. A bored bunny tends to be lethargic, may eat more, groom herself more frequently and is also more likely to be destructive if it helps to keep her occupied.

Foster bunny Charlie is famous for shredding junk mail and magazines.

Toys are very important for your rabbit's physical and mental well-being. They will keep her active and interested in her surroundings and help her live longer (overweight, bored bunnies usually die young). However, toys are not just for rabbits, they also protect your home while keeping your rabbit stimulated.

You may need to try different toys before you find something your bunny likes. Moving things around and providing new toys from time to time will help to keep your pet busy and happy. You can give your rabbit the following:

- Items made of untreated straw and other natural fibres (seagrass, maize, wicker, and so on) for nibbling or scratching. You can buy mats, baskets, coasters, bags, hats, wastepaper bins and even brooms very cheaply in many high street shops and they usually keep a bunny occupied for hours.
- Big paper bags for crawling in, scratching and chewing.
- Cat toys, for example plastic or wire balls with a bell inside, and other toys that roll or can be tossed.
- Hard plastic baby rattles. Avoid teething rings and other items made of soft plastic which your rabbit could nibble at.
- Cardboard rolls from paper towels or toilet paper for tossing, rolling and chewing. If you stand them up on the floor your rabbit can push them down with her muzzle.
- Hard plastic balls for nudging and chasing.
- Dried out pine cones.
- A flannel or knotted piece of towelling for lifting and tossing.
- Yoghurt pots or paper cups which your bunny can pick up and throw. These are also good for human-stacks-on-the-floor and bunny-knocks-them-down type of games.
- Hard plastic caps from softener bottles or bubble bath containers

Spok and Ayosha often lie under their favourite chair.

Charlie gives his new toys the seal of approval.

Flip-Flop is not much bigger than his favourite toy.

33

for picking up and tossing. Don't use caps from bathroom cleaner bottles and other caustic materials and do them wash very thoroughly before giving to your rabbit.

- Children's toys covered in towelling or fabric (perhaps a small rag doll) for lifting and tossing.
- A fluffy toy or furry slipper to snuggle up to (remove if bunny chews).
- Things your rabbit can tear up and scratch. These might include old magazines and newspapers, paper bags, last year's phone book or Yellow Pages, an empty tissue box, egg cartons or even your junk mail.
- Parrot toys that can be tossed or hung under a table for chewing or hitting.
- Untreated wood, twigs and branches which have been aged for three months or more. You can give your bunny willow or apple tree twigs straight from the tree. Avoid redwood, apricot, cherry, peach and plum, which are poisonous to rabbits.

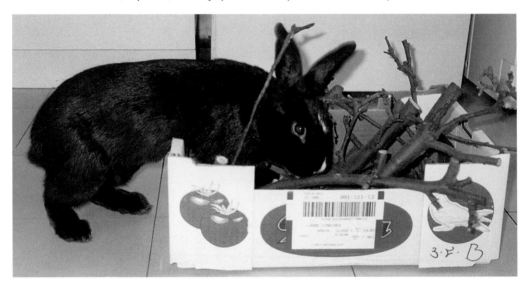

Woolly soon finds the new box of twigs.

- Cardboard boxes from your supermarket, such as nappy boxes. Tape them closed and cut two or more windows for hopping in and out. Many rabbits don't like boxes with just one opening because they don't feel safe (in the wild burrows have more than one exit hole). If you leave the bottom or side of each flap attached to the box your bunny can finish opening it on her own if she wants to.
- You can buy boxes of all shapes and sizes and some made of thick corrugated cardboard from packing shops (useful if you need a "made-to-measure" box for your pet). Create an interesting bunny play area by lining some of the boxes (with newspaper, carpet squares, old towels, natural fibre mats) or filling them (with shredded paper, hay and straw).

- One or two wooden boxes made of 12 mm plywood. Ask your timberyard to cut the wood to the right size and saw two or more windows in the side walls, depending on how big the box is. As you assemble the box, remember to hinge rather than nail the roof panel (this will make cleaning out easier).

Isobel ventures from her basket to investigate a new toy.

- A wooden tunnel made with four lengths of ½ inch (12mm) plywood (each measuring 1ft x 2ft (30cm x 61cm) or 1ft x 3ft (30cm x 91cm)).
- A big cardboard poster tube from a stationer or art supplies shop.
- A natural straw or wicker basket, for example, a baby carrier. Line it with a bin bag and newspaper and fill with hay and straw so your rabbit can dig, have a snack and do her business at the same time.
- A low, non-slippery table and one or two chairs for climbing on. Put a towel or cushion on the seat of the chair so your bunny doesn't slip. Provided your bunny is litter-trained it's alright to let her hop on the sofa and play with the cushions.
- A wooden shelf for vertical jumps.
- Cat toys with ramps, tunnels, tubes and look-outs.
- Your rabbit's travel cage for hopping in and out. Put in a carrot or other treat or fill it with hay and straw so your bunny doesn't associate it with unpleasant things (like going to the vet).

A travelling basket can be used for trips or going to/from the garden.

chapter 6

The Early Days

Large rabbits such as Snowy, Ayosha and Clementine tend to be more laid-back than the smaller varieties........

Any rabbit can be the right rabbit: male or female, big or small, baby or adult. With over 75 breeds to choose from, and some delightful crossbreeds, you are bound to find a bunny that appeals to you. Cashmere, Angora and other long-haired rabbits require a lot of care and grooming and should only be taken on by very dedicated people.

Contrary to popular belief, large rabbits are better for children because they will be less likely to pick up and drop them. Larger breeds also tend to be more placid and laid-back than small rabbits like Netherland Dwarfs. However, they do require a bigger pen and exercise area.

If you are planning to have a house rabbit, it is better to adopt one who is over a year old as she'll be less destructive around the home. Rabbits can be house-trained at any age, so there's no need to worry that an adult rabbit will not learn to use a litter tray.

Many people think that if they buy a baby rabbit and handle her often, she will enjoy being picked up and mothered. This is rarely the case as most baby bunnies are far too busy dashing around and exploring their environment to be held for long. Rabbits of any age can become tame and affectionate if they are petted on their own terms (at floor level) and you are willing to put in the time.

Adopting A Rabbit From A Rescue Centre

The best place to get a rabbit is your local animal shelter. Every year, thousands of unwanted pet rabbits end up at rescue centres across the country. When you adopt from a rescue centre you are giving a second chance to a rabbit in need. In addition, you will enable the shelter to take in another rabbit who would otherwise have to be turned away or put to sleep. (See Resources on page 94 for details of your local shelter.)

.......however, they will require more spacious accommodation and pen area.

Taking Your Rabbit Home

You can collect your rabbit from the shelter in a travel cage or a strong cardboard box with ventilation holes, lined with newspaper, hay and straw. Remember that this is a big day for your rabbit; she will be much happier if you take her straight home so she can settle as quickly as possible. You should have everything you need before you take your new pet home including her bed and living area.

Your rabbit will probably urinate in her box on the way home. Pad the box well because, if the cardboard becomes saturated, it will no longer hold the weight of the rabbit. If you are travelling by car or train, rest the box on your lap so the rabbit doesn't get thrown about and talk to her in a soft tone of voice. Don't pass the box from one person to the other or you will frighten your new rabbit. Never leave the rabbit in the boot of the car, on the floor near the air conditioning vent, or in a sunny place because she may get heatstroke. If your rabbit is in an open cardboard box remember to keep all car windows closed. Rabbits can sense open spaces and may suddenly leap from the box out of the car.

Avoid making a lot of noise or playing loud music on the way home, particularly if the bunny was used to living in a quiet place.

Once your new bunny starts to eat, you will know that she is settling in.

Once home...

As soon as you get home, put your bunny in her cage or bed and don't disturb her for a while. It is vital that she has the chance to recover from the journey and get used to her new environment. Picking her up or even petting her will only worry her at this point. Just sit quietly in the room and let the bunny sniff everything in peace and mark her territory. When she starts eating and grooming herself and maybe rolling on her back, you'll know she has overcome the initial shock.

Talk to your bunny softly from time to time, so she gets used to the sound of your voice. If you repeat her name often she will recognise it after a few days.

It is probably better to leave the rabbit in her pen for the first day, where she feels safe and has access to her toys and litter tray. On the second day you can let her hop around a room or the part of it that has been prepared for her. This should contain at least one litter tray, a digging box, one or two cardboard boxes, chew and toss toys. Allow your bunny to explore only one room at a time or she will feel insecure and forget where the litter trays are. Wait a few days before introducing her to your

Senior foster bunny Spok settles in his new home.

relatives and friends, and other family pets.

The first days indoors

Even if you intend to let your rabbit hop around the entire house, it's a good idea to start with just one room without carpet or wallpaper such as the kitchen, bathroom, hallway or boxroom. This should be carefully rabbit-proofed and furnished with the same items you put in the pen - chew/toss toys, a rug, litter tray, some large baskets, cardboard boxes, seagrass mats, carpet squares and so on. Gradually increase your rabbit's space by one room at a time.

Rather than closing the door on your bunny, install a baby gate so she can see

This seagrass mat will keep Carolina occupied for a while.

and hear you while she's in her room. Make sure she can't squeeze herself between the bars or jump over it - if necessary you may have to build a taller gate with wire mesh tacked onto a wooden frame. Minimum recommended height is 3ft (91cm) or 4ft (1.2m) for very athletic bunnies.

Natural seagrass mats can be used to protect your carpet and provide both chewing and digging material.

In the first few days, it is probably better not to clean the bunny's pen and litter trays too thoroughly so she can recognise them as her own. If the litter tray is always clean the bunny might think it is supposed to be that way and may start using something else as her toilet.

Children in the family will be very excited at the new arrival and will want to play with her straight away. Gently explain to them that they must wait a few days before petting and brushing the rabbit and that only adults are allowed to pick her up.

After a few days the bunny will become more relaxed and will probably come and sniff your hand and greet you. When this happens she is ready to meet other household members.

To introduce your bunny to a group of people, have everyone sit in a circle around her allotted space (close doors leading to other rooms). Rabbits are inquisitive by nature and your bunny will go up to each individual to sniff him and chin him. When this happens that person should slowly put a hand in front of the bunny, reaching down from above. If the bunny remains in front of your hand, you may try petting her very gently - but stop if she looks anxious or annoyed. Don't stroke your rabbit's coat in the wrong direction or try to pick her up in the early days.

Repeat these sessions daily until the rabbit does not show any fear and accepts petting from everyone. When a bunny lies still it doesn't necessarily mean she wants to be petted, so everyone should learn to distinguish between relaxed crouching and the freeze posture. When a rabbit is tense you can see the white in the corner of her eyes. Do not try to pet her; talk to her in a comforting voice. If she looks very relaxed and perhaps lowers her head, she is inviting you to give her a cuddle.

In the early days, your bunny may mark her territory with lots of urine and pellets. This will improve as the bunny gets into the habit of using her litter trays.

When you take home a new rabbit, move slowly and quietly and give her a chance to find her bearings. If you have a small rabbit, she will probably try to squeeze between and behind furniture or hide under beds and other hard-to-reach places. Make sure all cables in these areas are protected and, if necessary, use telephone directories and other items to block the gaps behind the cooker, fridge and other appliances.

Rabbits quickly learn to hop up and down two or three steps and, in some cases, will confidently go down a full flight of stairs. Other bunnies, however, are afraid of falling on their way down and prefer to wait on the landing to be 'rescued'. A simple but effective way to prevent this is to install a baby gate at the bottom of the stairs. I use a similar gate to stop my rabbit from hopping into the garden if I don't have time to supervise her.

Finally, don't plan an outing or a visit to friends with your bunny during the first few days. Too many new sights and experiences would confuse and intimidate your rabbit.

Befriending A Rabbit

Friendship with your rabbit begins by spending some time with her every day. This is more likely to happen if the rabbit lives indoors with you rather than in the garden. Let your bunny approach you while you sit in her running space, reading or watching tv. Rabbits are naturally curious and will come up to you to investigate. If the rabbit doesn't run away you can try to pet her on the forehead, ears and back. Remember to approach the bunny from above, not below eye level, or she may perceive your hand as threatening. Rabbits don't like having their chin, feet or tail touched.

As your bunny comes to enjoy the feeling of being stroked, you may try to brush her, comb her or give her a back scratch. Again, confine yourself to the top of the head, ears and back. Soon your bunny will start begging you to be stroked and groomed.

Your rabbit may not want to be held in your lap. When you sit on the floor or sofa, she may hop on your lap for a moment. Spreading a towel across your lap will make it more inviting to her and protect you from scratches. Let your rabbit hop on and off your lap of her own accord.

Picking Up A Rabbit

Contrary to popular belief, the vast majority of rabbits don't like to be held and prefer to sit next to you when you pet them. However there are times when you have to pick up your rabbit, for instance to take her to the vet. For this reason it's a good idea to practise lifting and setting her down every day. Follow this exercise with a reward so your bunny will come to see it as a positive experience.

To pick up a large rabbit, put one hand under her chest and the other under her bottom, then lift the bunny facing away from you. Remember to act confidently or your rabbit will sense your hesitation. Rabbits can break their spine if they kick out suddenly, so hold the back legs firmly in your hand.

To pick up a small rabbit, put one hand under her forelegs and one under her bottom and scoop towards you. Hold the bunny securely against your body to prevent her from kicking.

Picking up a rabbit by the scruff of the neck is not recommended because it may cause tissue damage. Most rabbits are far too heavy to be lifted in this way and a lot of them don't even have much loose skin with which to pick them up.

Take care when setting a bunny down, as she may leap in anticipation. The best method is to bend your legs and quickly release her. Many adults find it difficult to keep hold of a struggling bunny, so we don't recommend letting children pick up a rabbit for their own safety and that of the bunny.

Pick your bunny up by placing one hand under his forelegs and the other under his bottom.

chapter 7

Litter and Litter training

Hay is a good choice for the litter tray.

It is important to fill your rabbit's litter tray with a non-toxic, absorbent litter. Most rabbits try to chew the litter or will ingest some during grooming. If the litter isn't absorbent the urine may splash back on the rabbit, causing urine burn. Avoid dusty/clumping clay litters and softwood litters which can be harmful to your pet.

It is a good idea to try several types of litter to find which one your rabbit likes best. Many rabbits like digging and rolling in the litter. Use a soft litter if your bunny tends to have sore hocks or spends a lot of time in her litter tray.

Other choices will depend on individual rabbits. If your rabbit tends to chew on the litter, it is better to use an organic variety but change the tray frequently to prevent mould. Even then, you don't want your bunny to ingest large amounts of litter. If you have purchased one that your rabbit finds too tasty, try another variety.

Lightweight litter is easier to use but tends to track more. Also, if your bunny likes dragging the litter tray around the room, it is better to use a heavier litter or secure the litter tray to a piece of furniture.

Meadow hay/straw

With a thick layer of newspapers underneath, this is one of the cheapest and most widely available litters. We use it to encourage some rabbits to eat more hay and straw, which are essential to a healthy digestive system. When the litter is soiled, you can simply roll up the newspaper and throw it away.

This type of litter tends to be messy and should be put in a tray with high sides or a plastic dog bed/storage box to keep it contained. The sharp seed husks of barley

Some bunnies like to sleep in their litter tray.

Now that's what I call a high-sided litter tray!

straw can sometimes injure the rabbit's paws so do shake them out before placing in the litterbox. Dust-extracted hay and straw free of mites and mould are available in bales and mini-bales from some manufacturers. Hay and straw can be composted in the garden.

Dried grass
This can also be used as litter but it's more expensive and nutritious than hay or straw.

Chopped barley straw
This is very similar in appearance and consistency to wood shavings and is a bit messy for indoor use. The small particles may irritate the bunny's eyes and respiratory system.

Pelleted straw litter
This is absorbent, breaks down when wet and can easily be disposed of in the garden. The litter has a natural fragrance that helps to disguise the smell of urine.

Peat/garden soil
This is quite absorbent but looks a bit 'dirty' indoors. It also tends to cling to the fur and is then carried around the house by the bunny. Rabbits love to dig and roll in compost so we keep it in a large tray in the garden.

Corncob litter
This has a pleasant smell and is fairly absorbent. However it is very expensive and may make your rabbit put on weight if it is ingested. Like other organic litters it can become mouldy so change the trays frequently (mould is toxic to rabbits).

Recycled paper litter
Like the one made for cats, this is available in flakes or pellets. It is lightweight, dust-free and absorbent but take care that the rabbit doesn't swallow large quantities. Recycled paper does not support mould or bacterial growth.

Shredded newspaper

I have found this to be less absorbent but adequate as long as the bunny doesn't chew on it. We sometimes use it in our rabbits' digging boxes.

Plain newspaper is not recommended. It is not very absorbent and the rabbit may step on her urine, splashing it on her legs and genital area. This may result in urine burn, particularly if the rabbit cannot reach to clean herself (because she is overweight or has a large dewlap). Paper-trained rabbits will also tend to urinate on every magazine or sheet of paper you leave

Dorothy loves to spend time on her pelleted straw litter.

lying around. However, disabled bunnies who are unable to hop in the litter tray may be taught to use newspaper covered with a few sheets of kitchen roll.

Paper pulp bedding

This is a natural litter made from reclaimed wood fibres that are too short to be used in paper production. This bedding is very absorbent and controls odour beautifully. It is lightweight and easy to carry. It doesn't contaminate wounds, making it ideal for post-operative care and rabbits suffering from sore hocks, sensitive skin and so on. It is sanitised to kill bacteria, mould and fungus and won't harm your pet if eaten. It has no added inks, dyes or other chemicals, unlike recycled paper litters. Paper litter won't scratch floors, it can be vacuumed up, flushed, composted and is biodegradable.

Clumping cat litter

This is not recommended for rabbits. It is generally made of a substance called sodium bentonite, a naturally swelling clay. When liquid is added, bentonite swells to approximately 15 times its original volume. Rabbits are very clean animals and, when they groom, they ingest small particles of litter. Once the clay is inside the rabbit it expands, forming a mass and coating the digestive tract. This causes dehydration, both by drawing fluids from the rabbit and preventing the absorption of nutrients and other liquids. As a result the rabbit may develop diarrhoea (in an attempt to cleanse her system), an internal blockage or even die.

Clumping clay litter also produces a fine dust when stirred (when it's being poured into the tray or a bunny digs in the litter). Clay dust may cause cancer and respiratory disease if inhaled over a period of time. It can also irritate the eyes and is harmful to both humans and rabbits.

Bits of litter which are kicked out of the tray may scratch wooden or linoleum floors. Clay litter is heavy and isn't suitable for garden compost.

Other cat litters

Non-clumping, dust-free cat litters are a safer choice for your rabbit. They are lighter than ordinary clay and are available from pet shops and supermarkets.

Softwood Litters

Studies from as far back as 1967 have shown that softwood beddings (for example pine shavings) can cause liver disease in small animals.

When you open a bag of softwood shavings you will immediately smell their fragrance. This is where the problem lies. The smell is from the natural volatile chemicals in the wood called phenols. Phenols are caustic, poisonous, acidic compounds which are routinely diluted for use in disinfectants, such as Jeyes Fluid. Inhaling phenols over time can irritate the mucous membranes of the nose and respiratory tract which, in turn, predisposes the rabbit to bacterial infection. The risk of damage to the liver and kidneys, however, is even more serious. As the principal organs for filtering blood and urine and eliminating toxins from them, the liver and kidneys are designed to process only a certain amount of toxic material. The most obvious consequence of regular exposure to large amounts of toxins such as phenols is that the body is working to its limit already and cannot cope with the added burden of anaesthetic. At lower levels, however, there may still be damage to the liver which is not fatal in itself but which is sufficient to depress the immune system, leaving the rabbit vulnerable to infections, particularly of the respiratory tract.

Fortunately this type of liver disease can be avoided by removing the softwood bedding from the environment. For a safer use of softwood litter, keep it in large, open, well-ventilated areas only and have your rabbit's blood checked every few months. Finally, the dust contained in softwood litter (particularly sawdust and shavings) can irritate a rabbit's eyes.

Litter training your pet bunny

Rabbits are very clean animals - in the wild they only use certain places to relieve themselves and don't soil inside their warrens. Pet bunnies also tend to go to the toilet in just one or a few places and are easy to house-train.

Some rabbits litter train themselves but most need a little encouragement from their owners. Rabbits usually learn to urinate in a litter tray but will still scatter a few droppings around. This is normal rabbit behaviour and the little brown pellets are easy to pick up and discard and can also be vacuumed.

Rabbits can be house-trained from just a few weeks of age; those over a year old are often easier to train, especially if they have been neutered. Neutering is very important if your rabbit lives in the house. When a rabbit is growing up she becomes very restless and territorial marking with urine and droppings will increase. Even litter trained bunnies start urinating outside their trays and this may happen every spring if your bunny hasn't been neutered. Neutering will make your rabbit more reliably trained and will also prevent or reduce spraying.

To litter train your bunny, you will need at least one litter tray. Buy one with low sides for a small or baby rabbit; for a larger bunny get a big tray like the ones used by small dogs or take the bottom pan of a bird cage.

You should get your bunny used to the litter tray from the very first day; this means having a couple of litter trays ready when you first bring your bunny home. If you have more than one tray you'll increase your bunny's chances of getting things right. Later you can remove the trays your rabbit uses less frequently.

I suggest you start with one room, even if you plan to give your rabbit full run of the house - if she has too much to explore, she'll be overwhelmed and forget where her toilet is. Choose the kitchen or another room without carpet. If all your rooms are carpeted, use a smaller room so that your rabbit is more likely to find the tray.

Put a litter tray in the rabbit's pen or near her bed and maybe a second in a corner of the room. Put a few pellets and a piece of urine-soaked tissue in the tray(s) so your rabbit gets the message. Make sure you show your rabbit where you have put the tray(s). If she hops in, offer her a treat and lots of praise. Otherwise, herd her gently towards the tray or entice her there with a titbit.

Rabbits are more likely to go in the tray if you make it an attractive place to be. Leave a handful of hay or your rabbit's food dish in one corner. Experiment with different types of litter to find the one your bunny prefers. Many rabbits enjoy digging and rolling in their trays, grooming or even sleeping. This should be encouraged because if your rabbit likes spending time in her tray she's more likely to mark it with urine and droppings.

Placing her food dish in the litter tray will encourage your rabbit to frequent it.

In the beginning it's a good idea to watch your bunny during her free-running time so if she starts urinating in the wrong places you can hopefully break the habit before it becomes established. If you see your bunny pushing her tail and bottom out, she is probably about to urinate. If your rabbit is in the tray, wait until she has finished and give her lots of praise and a nice pat. A treat will also help to make your bunny feel good so hopefully she will want to repeat the experience.

If your rabbit isn't in the tray, clap your hands twice to get her attention and say "No, X" firmly but without shouting. Then pick up your rabbit and put her in the litter tray. If she doesn't like to be picked up, lure her there with a favourite treat. Never chase and grab your rabbit then put her in the litter tray or she will perceive this as punishment. Once your rabbit is inside the tray give her the treat and lots of praise. Be patient if your rabbit doesn't understand and urinates on the floor - house-training doesn't happen in one day and may take several weeks, especially if the bunny hasn't been neutered yet.

Many rabbits prefer finding their own place for depositing their urine and droppings. Simply move the litter tray where they need it. If their chosen spot is not convenient, once they have got used to urinating in the tray you can gradually move it to where you want it to be.

As your rabbit becomes more reliable, you can allow her in the rest of the house, one room at a time. I would recommend you place a litter tray in every room your bunny has access to, at least in the early days. When you go out leave your rabbit in the kitchen (or another uncarpeted room) to limit the number of "accidents" until training is complete.

Scolding your rabbit has no place in litter training. It is acceptable to use the word "No" without shouting but you must do so immediately after the bunny has urinated on the floor. Needless to say, you should never smack your rabbit or swat her with a newspaper, no matter how gently. This will not help in the slightest and will traumatise your new rabbit.

Cleaning up

For cleaning up litter training accidents, the cheapest and most effective way is to use diluted white vinegar. This can be used on carpets, lino floors, painted floorboards, and so on. Use it in its undiluted form to remove stubborn stains from floors and litter trays.

Litter trays should usually be cleaned daily. Ammonia fumes from the urine can trigger off respiratory infections, so discard dirty litter frequently.

chapter 8

Preventing Destructive Behaviour

Chewing and digging are normal activities for a rabbit, especially during adolescence. Neutering will help to reduce this behaviour, however rabbits still need to chew, dig, and explore their territory. It is therefore our responsibility to meet these needs in ways that don't cause damage to our home. As a bunny gets older, she will tend to become less destructive and easier to manage, especially if she's neutered.

Chewing

A rabbit's front teeth continue to grow throughout her lifetime, so she constantly needs to keep them in trim. In addition to food rabbits enjoy nibbling on other items to experience their taste and texture, to develop strong jaw muscles or simply to keep themselves busy.

Excessive chewing may also be a sign that the rabbit wants attention. Is your rabbit left alone for several hours at a time? Would a friend relieve boredom? Anything that would keep your rabbit happy and occupied might reduce chewing.

The first step in preventing destructive behaviour is to bunny-proof your house. Confining your rabbit to one or two small, well bunny-proofed rooms (or to a large pen when you are not at home) will help to limit the damage until your bunny gets older or you have her neutered.

Widget playing with a selection of toys.

Next, you should provide your rabbit with a variety of chew toys to divert her attention from furniture and carpets. The most useful are those items made of wood, cardboard and untreated straw/seagrass. A rabbit who only has a piece of wood and a branch to gnaw on quickly becomes bored and is more likely to be destructive. You can train a rabbit not to chew on something by saying the word "No" followed by her name and immediately offering her something she is allowed to chew. If possible, provide items with a similar or

Tired out from play, Snoopy dozes in his pen.

better texture, such as a piece of plain untreated wood instead of the skirting board, a carpet square or straw mat instead of the carpet, or an apple twig instead of furniture legs. You can also spray chew repellents (made for puppies and kittens) on your furniture and other items daily until the rabbit stops trying to chew them.

If your bunny is confined to a pen or a small room, leave a few coasters and small baskets in her territory so she gets used to nibbling on her toys while you are not at home. When she is let out of her pen, she will find the larger straw mats and baskets and will know what to do with them. If your rabbit doesn't get the idea, keep removing her from unsuitable objects and gently place her on her mat or in front of a basket. Make sure fresh hay, straw and one or two twigs are always available. Be consistent so your rabbit quickly learns what is acceptable behaviour. Above all, never raise your voice or smack your rabbit as this will terrify her.

Excessive chewing

Rabbits usually tend to leave what they chew in shreds on the floor. However, if your bunny gets into the habit of swallowing the likes of carpet, paper and cardboard, you should give her plenty of hay and straw and also a petroleum laxative from the pet shop. If your bunny is unwell, take her to the vet immediately.

Burrowing/digging

Rabbits need to dig to wear down their toenails, which grow continuously, especially the nails on their front feet. If your bunny doesn't have much opportunity to dig or hop

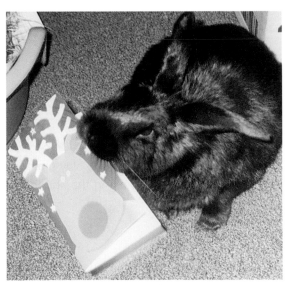

Carolina recycling a Christmas card.

A wicker basket filled with cones and toys.

Wooden tunnels can also be used for sitting on.

on hard surfaces (for example concrete or patio tiles), you should check her nails frequently and clip them if necessary. Bunnies with long nails are more likely to dig in the carpet or on your bed.

Most rabbits enjoy digging in corners and at the end of tunnels. Others will dig anywhere they can, for example on the sofa, by a door or in the middle of a room. If there is a certain place on the carpet where your rabbit likes to dig, cover it with furniture, a carpet square (held down with furniture) or a straw mat. Offer a digging box as well, such as a large plastic tub, wicker basket or cardboard/wooden box filled with hay, straw, corncob, shredded paper, old magazines, egg cartons, towels and so on.

Cardboard concrete forms from building supply stores make appealing and inexpensive edible tunnels. Encourage your bunny to dig by putting some newspaper or an old phone book at the far end. If your rabbit prefers to doze off rather than dig in a tunnel, you can get cat tunnels lined with carpet or synthetic fleece. These are very comfortable and appeal to the majority of bunnies. Alternatively, give your rabbit a long, narrow cardboard box, a linen basket or a wooden tunnel open at both ends. For the garden, invest in a large clay pipe or build a tunnel with water-proof plywood.

Female rabbits often dig in the soil to make a burrow, especially when they are going through a false pregnancy. Again, neutering will help reduce this behaviour. If your rabbit is a keen burrower, make sure she doesn't dig her way out of the garden. Always fill in the hole at the end of the day and bury the wire netting at least 16-20 inches (40-50cm) into the ground. It is probably safer to build a large run with a wire mesh bottom covered with hay and straw for digging. A large tub or litter tray full of sand/compost can be left outside to provide a digging area for your bunny.

chapter 9

Understanding Your Rabbit

Rabbits are sociable creatures who should not live on their own. If you are away from home during the day it is essential to get your house rabbit a companion or she will be lonely and bored. Loneliness can also lead to excessive destructiveness and loss of litter-training.

Isobel and Pebbles enjoying each other's company.

Introducing Rabbits

Introducing another rabbit to your household enables your existing bunny to have a friend when you are not around. Two rabbits together will share food, water, litter trays, toys, rugs and sleeping areas so they are more or less the same work as having one bunny. Some people believe if they have two rabbits they will be less friendly towards humans. However, rabbits love being with people and, if anything, they'll be even more affectionate towards you because they are more content. In addition I've found that in a pair the more timid bunny will eventually take after the more confident rabbit and she too will become friendlier towards people.

Introducing two or more rabbits can take a few weeks or months but it is definitely worth the effort because, in the end, your bunny will have a companion for life. Introductions can be stressful for rabbits so take your time and proceed very slowly.

Also be prepared for loss of litter training, as the bunnies frantically mark their territory. This should settle once the bunnies become friends. Three or more rabbits are messier than just one or two so, unless you have set up the right environment (without carpet) and are prepared to do quite a bit of cleaning up, we do not recommend keeping more than three free-range house rabbits in the same area.

Tiger and Peanut.

Before you even consider introducing two rabbits of the opposite sex, you must ensure they are both neutered in order to prevent excessive fighting and/or unwanted babies. Wait until the stitches are removed about 10 days after the neutering operation - this is particularly important if your female bunny has just been spayed as mounting by a male could cause internal damage.

If you already have one rabbit it is easier to introduce another neutered rabbit of the opposite sex. Usually there will be less fighting if you bring a female bunny home to a male rather than vice versa. This is because female rabbits tend to be very protective of their immediate territory (their cage, room, and so on) and are generally more aggressive towards newcomers. Two rabbits of the same sex can also live happily together, especially if they are females. It is harder for male bunnies to become friends, but not impossible. Neutering is, once again, essential even if the rabbits are of the same sex and there's no danger of breeding. Rabbits who are not neutered may start fighting without any warning and cause terrible injuries to each other. If you wait until this happens to get your rabbits neutered, it is then usually too late to restore their friendship.

Before introducing any animals, it is important to let them sniff each other for a few days (perhaps through a baby gate) so they can get used to each other's scent. Take care not to neglect existing pets in favour of the new rabbit or they will be jealous and become more aggressive towards the newcomer.

Introductions should always take place on neutral territory (for example in a bathtub, a child's playpen, an unfamiliar room or a friend's house). If you cannot offer neutral territory then make sure you provide a large one (the garden is useful) so, if necessary, one bunny can get away from the other. It is normal for bunnies to fight at the beginning, so be prepared to break up fights by squirting the aggressive rabbit with warm water or by making a loud noise to stop them in their tracks; for instance you could clap your hands, thump the floor or turn on a portable vacuum cleaner.

New friends Benjamin and Lucy snuggle up together.

When introducing two rabbits, it is important to differentiate between scuffles and vicious fighting. Fur flying, chasing, sexual behaviour and nipping are all normal in an introduction and you should not immediately rush to separate your rabbits. However, be prepared to intervene if things become too rough. To minimise injuries, wear oven gloves to protect yourself, make sure your rabbits' nails are trimmed short and that there are no sharp pieces of furniture your rabbits could run into when fighting or chasing each other.

Slowly increase the time your bunnies spend together from a few seconds/minutes to a few hours until you are confident your rabbits can be kept together without fighting. Taking your bunnies on car trips for 15 minutes or so every day will make them want to snuggle up together rather than fight and can be very useful in speeding up introductions. Wait until the engine is running and place the two travel cages on the back seat. Open the carrier doors and you will find that the rabbits tend to snuggle up together. After a few car trips you may be able to keep the bunnies together in a neutral room afterwards.

Rabbits can become friends with well-behaved dogs. First, it is vital your dog understands and obeys some basic commands such as "No", "Stay" and "Gentle". Get your dog used to seeing the rabbit hopping around freely - you could do this by putting your dog in a puppy pen and letting the rabbit have the run of the room. Or put the dog on a harness and lead and be prepared to hold him back if he tries to attack the rabbit. Introducing your rabbit to a dog is more likely to succeed if your rabbit is confident and not easily frightened.

Cat-rabbit introductions are usually successful if the rabbit is not overly timid and if both animals are adults. A young kitten may be too boisterous for a bunny and a baby rabbit (rat-size) is more likely to be seen as prey by a cat.

Rabbits can live happily with guinea pigs, but this is not always the case. Again, it is essential you have your rabbit neutered so she doesn't harass the guinea pig. Make sure their living quarters are as big as possible and that the guinea pig has a hiding place he can retreat to. Look out for signs of bullying, for example the rabbit preventing the guinea pig from accessing the food bowl. Some guinea pigs have also been known to scratch and injure rabbits, so watch out for these signs as well.

With any introductions, take things slowly and be prepared to house the newcomer in separate accommodation until the introduction is over. Avoid introducing a new rabbit to other pets for a week or so to enable the bunny to become familiar with her surroundings first. And, of course, never leave your pets alone unsupervised until you are certain they will not attack each other.

Body Language And Behaviour

Rabbits use body language to communicate their moods and thoughts to people, rabbits and other animals. Rabbits are gentler and more understated than other pets so learning about their behaviour requires time and patience. Most rabbit "words" are transmitted through movement, body posture and facial expression. Observe your rabbit and you will soon discover what she is doing or trying to say. The more you learn about her behaviour, the more responsive and charming your rabbit will become.

Apathy

Some rabbits are laid-back by nature, depending on the breed, and small rabbits are often more energetic than larger bunnies. A rabbit may spend a lot of time sleeping or lying down if she is ill, overweight or she feels uncomfortable (for example, if she has sore skin and matted fur under her tail).

In many cases what seems like a lazy or apathetic bunny may simply be one who is bored and in need of stimulation (in the form of toys, increased running space and more exercise). My house rabbit is normally quiet but, when I buy her a new toy or we have guests, she suddenly becomes very lively. Providing stimulation will keep your rabbit active and interested in her surroundings. A rabbit will tend to be more active if she has an animal friend to play with and

Older rabbits sleep more than their younger counterparts.

follow around. It is normal for a rabbit to become slower and sleep more as she gets older.

Assertive gestures

Rabbits are usually considered gentle and timid so it often comes as a surprise when a rabbit bites. In the vast majority of cases aggression has a behavioural, not a genetic, cause. So before you label your rabbit 'aggressive', try to understand what the problem is.

The following are some of the reasons why rabbits become aggressive:

- Sexual behaviour. Running around your feet, mounting and biting are usually signs of a sexually frustrated rabbit. Neutering will greatly help to moderate or eliminate this behaviour.

- Possessiveness. Un-neutered rabbits (especially females) can be very territorial, so it is best to clean their pen, food bowl and so on when they are not looking.

- Testing. It is common for young rabbits to try everything with their teeth. If your new bunny nips you, let out a small shriek to let her know that it hurt. That is the sound a rabbit would make when she's in pain.

- Move over. Rabbits will nip people, guinea pigs and other animals that are in their way. Make a short screech and avoid using your body as a barrier to restrain your rabbit.

- Boredom/frustration. Rabbits who don't get enough exercise or stimulation (in the form of company, toys, a varied diet and so on) are more likely to be aggressive.

- Misdirection. You may get bitten when you try to separate fighting rabbits or when you carry the smell of another rabbit on your clothing.

- Jealousy. Take care not to neglect your bunny when you introduce other animals into your home.

- Fear of heights or being dropped. Most rabbits do not feel secure when they're being held and may scratch and bite to get away.

- Enthusiastic grooming. When they groom one another, rabbits remove bits of dirt stuck in each other's fur. Don't be surprised if your rabbit nips you when she licks your sleeve or trousers and finds a button or seam that might be considered removable.

- Smelly fingers. Wash your hands after eating food so that your rabbit is not tempted to taste you! When handfeeding your bunny, hold a treat in the flat, outstretched palm of your hand and not between your fingers. Rabbits can't see well in front of their noses and may mistake your fingers for food.

- Fear/pain. A rabbit may become aggressive when she is sick or being given medication.

- Defence. Rabbits find objects coming from below threatening. Avoid putting your hand in front of a rabbit's nose to be sniffed as you would with a dog. When reaching into her cage, always approach a bunny from above, especially if your rabbit is timid and easily frightened.

- Abuse from humans. Rabbits who have been badly treated may become very aggressive towards people. The best way of coping with this situation is to treat aggression with benevolence. Wear protective clothing (long sleeves, gloves, shoes and so on) when approaching your rabbit. Give her her favourite food and lots of cuddles and praise. Eventually she will associate you with positive things, and will stop attacking you. Making friends with an aggressive rabbit takes a lot of time and patience but is very rewarding.

Backward mounting

A sexually inexperienced bunny may try to mate with his partner's head instead of the bottom end. When this happens there is always the risk that the rabbit underneath will bite the other's genitals, so you should separate them as soon as possible.

Chinning

By rubbing their chin against plants, furniture and other items, rabbits mark them as their property. The special scent (undetectable to humans) is produced by a row of glands under the chin. Male rabbits have larger glands and do most of the chinning. Rabbits like to mark anything left on the floor, such as clothes, shoes and bags of shopping. My house rabbit immediately notices anything new around the house or garden and chins it accordingly. If a strange rabbit chins her possessions she becomes very restless and will seek out the intruder. Even friendly rabbits like to chin an object again after it has been marked by their companions to claim it once more as their own.

Circling

Circling your feet (or another rabbit) is part of the courtship ritual and means that your rabbit wants to mate. This is usually accompanied by soft cooing noises, spraying and mating your arms or legs. When this happens it is time to have your bunny neutered. Circling is also used to request food or attention. My bunny does this if I am near her food cupboard and she wants something to eat.

Bunnies can be very possessive about their homes and partners. When I looked after a friend's rabbit during the holidays, he would circle me whenever I cleaned his basket. I had to keep pushing him gently away and eventually he gave me a nip. I suggest you wait until a bunny is in her run or another room before you clean her bed or interfere with her possessions. As a rabbit gets to know you, or after she is neutered, she should become less territorial.

Copying

If you have more than one rabbit, you may have noticed that they adopt the other one's habits. Grooming, 'dancing', thumping, destructive and playful behaviour are some of the activities copied from other rabbits. When a bunny is afraid of something, other rabbits will also become frightened, for example at the vet's. Rabbits can learn by imitation, for example to drink from a bottle or use the cat flap. House rabbit fosterers who keep bunnies in groups pay little attention to house-training when introducing a new bunny because she will usually learn from the others.

Dancing

Leaping and running at high speed are a rabbit's way of enjoying her freedom and also a sign that she feels happy and at home in her surroundings. Bunny aerobics are a joy to watch and include athletic jumps and spins in mid-air, zig-zagging, doubling back and forth and occasionally running into bushes and furniture.

Ears

A rabbit's ears are very sensitive to noise and can be pointed in different directions to listen to two sounds at once. When a bunny is curious about something, she points her ears toward the object of attention. Pulled back ears and a tense body may indicate the rabbit is about to attack. A bunny also lays back her ears when she is trying to appear inconspicuous.

Eating soft droppings

Eating the soft (caecal) pellets is natural and vital to your rabbit's health. These pellets are rich in protein and vitamin B and are usually taken directly from the anus. Caecal pellets are moist and shiny with a fairly strong smell. They are smaller than ordinary droppings, soft and usually come in clusters. If a rabbit produces a lot of soft droppings and does not re-ingest them it usually means her diet is too rich in protein and too low in fibre.

Fur-pulling

Rabbits chew their fur when they are bored, pining (after losing a partner) or when their skin is itchy. Pregnant or pseudo-pregnant females pluck the fur from their chest and tummy to make the nest. Fur-pulling is of course common during fights, for example amongst newly introduced rabbits.

Grooming/Licking

Rabbits keep themselves clean by licking their fur thoroughly several times a day. They also use grooming to show affection towards their human and animal friends. In an unfamiliar place, a bunny will groom herself once she feels comfortable and relaxed. If a rabbit is ill she will stop grooming her fur until she feels better.

Grooming may be used as a displacement activity when the bunny is afraid or is trying to ignore you. Excessive grooming may be a sign that the rabbit is bored.

Rabbits may lick your hand or feet to request attention or as a thank you after you've given them a cuddle or a treat. Many rabbits will automatically start licking when scratched in their favourite spot (usually the lower back, bottom or sides). When you want two rabbits to become friends, you can trick one bunny into grooming the other in this way.

Huddling together

Bonded rabbits spend a lot of time nuzzling side by side, nose to nose, or lying on top of each other.

A bunny who snuggles up to her human friends is also showing deep affection, especially if she does this without the enticement of petting or food.

Rabbits groom themselves thoroughly several times a day.

Indifference/Sulking

A rabbit may ignore you completely if she is angry with you, for instance if you've confined her to a room or show more affection towards another bunny. She may start grooming, turn her back on you or pretend to be interested in something else to avoid acknowledging your presence. Some rabbits will even sulk if you rearrange their cardboard boxes or other possessions.

Light nudging

Nudging your hand or leg may be a greeting (when you return home from work) or your rabbit's way of telling you she's nearby. It is also used to request attention and food. Some rabbits will nudge their owners two or three times in quick succession.

Lying flat on the ground with ears folded back

This is your bunny's way of hiding and becoming invisible when there's nowhere to hide. Wild rabbits do this when they are in danger or very frightened (if they've spotted a predator, for example). Look out if your bunny adopts this position indoors as she may break into a mad dash and bump into walls and furniture.

Making noise

A rabbit may toss objects such as her apple branch, toys or mineral lick to get attention. Making noise can also be a form of protest when the rabbit is hungry. For example, some rabbits tip over their food bowl or fling it across the room to demand more food. Other noisy activities include tearing up newspaper and cardboard boxes or thumping and shaking the baby gate to get attention.

Moving the jaws as if chewing

Rabbits sometimes do this when they're relaxed and content.

Nest-building

Un-neutered female rabbits make a nest when they are pregnant or going through a false pregnancy. They do this by gathering hay, straw, paper, tissues, socks or other material in a safe place and pulling the soft fur from their chest and belly. This behaviour may be accompanied by restlessness, mood changes and aggression. Pregnant females usually build the nest a couple of days before giving birth whilst non-pregnant females will do this around the 16th/17th day of their pseudo-pregnancy. Nesting behaviour is common in females even when they live on their own or with other females. It is stressful for your rabbit and can be prevented by having her spayed.

Nuzzling the head under another rabbit's chin

A rabbit pushes her head under another rabbit's chin when she's not very confident (for instance on meeting a strange rabbit) and wants to avoid a fight with a more dominant rabbit. If your new bunny lays her head down when you go near her, be especially gentle with her until she gains confidence. Rabbits also assume this posture to request petting from people or grooming from another rabbit.

Panting

Rabbits breathe very rapidly when they're hot or frightened. If your bunny is overweight, she may pant during exercise. Panting may also be a sign that your bunny is ill.

Pointing the muzzle and ears forward and stretching the tail

Rabbits do this when they are excited and interested in something, but wary as well for example when meeting an animal or person for the first time.

Pushing away your hand/leg

Forceful pushing away of your hand or other part of the body means that the rabbit has had enough of something (perhaps petting) or wants to get past. Some rabbits will even give you a nip if you don't move out of the way fast enough - discourage this type of behaviour by letting out a short screech to tell your bunny "That hurt!"

Rolling with eyes half closed

Rolling on her back or side means that the bunny feels happy and relaxed. Rabbits often do this after eating something good or after being petted. Rabbits also like to roll in their litter trays, sandboxes and dug up soil. If a bunny is very laid-back she may spend several minutes in this position and allow you to rub her tummy.

Shaking

If your hands smell of something strong - such as aftershave, disinfectant or household cleaner - when you pet your bunny, she may shake herself to get rid of the odour. Shaking also means the rabbit has had enough of something, perhaps being petted or brushed. A rabbit may also shake when she is ill or afraid. Some rabbits invite you to play with them by shaking their ears.

Shredding newspaper

Rabbits love tearing up paper and cardboard boxes while they play. Bored rabbits may do this to get attention and caged bunnies may do this in protest when they want to be let out for exercise.

Sitting quietly with eyes glazed over

If a rabbit sits huddled in a corner and refuses to move or eat, there's a chance that she may be ill or in pain. Other signs that she is not well include loud grinding of the teeth and looking straight ahead with dull eyes. Rabbits seldom whine or complain when they're suffering but can deteriorate and die very quickly without proper veterinary care. If in doubt, contact your vet immediately; waiting until the morning may be too late.

Periwinkle sits up to beg for attention.
Photo: Suzanne Pani

Standing up on the back feet

Rabbits stand on their hind legs to get a good view of their territory or to reach a favourite bit of food. They also stand up to beg for food or attention. If you see a bunny standing upright near a door it usually means she wants to be let in or out.

Stiff-legged posture

When a bunny wants to intimidate another, she may run past him with a stiff-legged posture. By raising her hindquarters and showing her tail the rabbit tries to appear bigger and more menacing. Usually she will move in decreasing semi-circles around the other rabbit and will attack if the other bunny doesn't retreat. During her parade the dominant rabbit might chin the ground or some small object in her path, scrape the floor or squirt urine on the other rabbit. The stiff-legged posture is also assumed by a male rabbit in the courtship ritual.

Tail movements

When a rabbit is relaxed you only see the tip of her tail. Rabbits raise their tail when they are curious and excited (for example, about food, a new object in their territory, a potential mate or an enemy approaching).

Courting rabbits and those who are fighting twitch their tails from side to side and spray their conquests with urine. A bold rabbit may switch her tail defiantly after doing something naughty (tearing the wallpaper, tipping over the wastepaper basket and so on). Some rabbits also twitch their tails as an invitation to play.

Marble was very nervous the first time he ventured into the garden.
Photo: Caroline Gilder

Tense posture with bulging eyes

When a bunny is worried about something, she crouches with eyes wide open and perks up her ears (unless she's a lop). This happens, for example, after she has heard a loud or unexpected noise. Cuddling your rabbit and talking to her quietly will help to relax her.

Rabbit Noises

Rabbits are usually quieter than other creatures but by no means silent. However, you have to listen very closely in order to hear them. Most rabbit sounds are soft and low - if a wild rabbit hopped around the countryside making loud noises she would soon attract the attention of predators.

Being quiet is one of the reasons why rabbits make such wonderful indoor companions. Having said that, they can also make a lot of noise when they play or to get attention (one example would be banging their food dish when dinner is late). Being individual, each bunny develops her own vocabulary of sounds to communicate with her carers. Rabbit noises can have different meanings, depending on the context.

Clucking

A pleasant sound is the soft clucking made by a rabbit who is eating her favourite treat. For example, my bunny does this while she nibbles on a piece of juicy pear, then licks her mouth and whiskers thoroughly.

Grunting

Male rabbits usually make a low nasal grunt after mating.

Honking

Honking and circling are part of the courtship behaviour and mean that a rabbit wants to mate. Even if your rabbit is neutered, she may continue to honk softly when she circles you or another rabbit.

Rabbits can also use this sound to request food or attention. My rabbit honks when she runs through her towel (her favourite game) or settles down for a nap.

Loud grinding of the teeth/crunching

Loud grinding of the teeth is very different from the soft gnashing described below. It denotes pain and discomfort, especially when combined with dull, bulging eyes and general apathy. If your bunny makes this sound, take her to the vet immediately.

Muttering/woofing

When I have a lie-in my rabbit, who knows I'm awake, mutters and paws at the mattress to request cuddles. If I don't pet her long enough, she immediately woofs to correct me for my mistake.

Sighing

My rabbit sighs when she has really had enough of something (having her fur clipped and so on).

Snorting/growling

When a rabbit is angry (for example if she's being chased), she may growl as a warning or just before an attack. This behaviour can be prevented or moderated by handling your rabbit correctly.

Soft grinding of the teeth/purring

This indicates that a bunny is very happy (perhaps while she's being massaged gently behind the ears). However, not all rabbits make this sound and some (including my own) grind their teeth very loudly when content (not to be confused with painful crunching). My bunny also rubs her teeth gently when she is comfortable and relaxed.

Soft moaning

Some rabbits moan gently when you pet them in the right spot, usually behind the ears and on the upper back.

Soft squeaking

Young rabbits sometimes squeak when they are hungry or frightened. A rabbit may also squeak softly when she takes the soft droppings from her bottom.

Squealing

Rabbits emit this cry when they are hurt or very scared, for example if they've been caught by a predator. When the bunny is in the garden it is essential to supervise her at all times to protect her from potential dangers (magpies, cats, dogs, foxes and so on). Not many people know that if a rabbit is very frightened she could die of a heart attack even before she is attacked.

Thumping

Rabbits stamp a back foot loudly on the ground when they are afraid of something. In the wild, rabbits thump to alert others that there is danger and give them a chance to dash to their burrows. The vibrations produced by thumping also warn the rabbits inside the burrows not to surface.

Stamping can also be a protest or threatening gesture - my rabbit never fails to thump at the veterinarian or when I am about to clip her nails. Rabbits may stamp their feet if they notice something out of the ordinary (a strange object, noise or smell), to make an announcement or simply to be noticed. Thumping is also a sign of sexual excitement, for instance when a male rabbit meets a new female rabbit.

Wheezing sniffs

Some rabbits express a protest with a combination of vocal and sniffing sounds.

Whimpering

Some rabbits make a fretting noise when you try to pick them up or when they don't want to be held any longer. A nervous bunny may whimper when you put your hand in her pen. When a rabbit is ill or in pain, she may also whine softly.

chapter 10

Sensory Capacities

Having many predators, wild rabbits are always alert to danger and use their sense organs to detect approaching enemies. Although she lives in the safety of your home, your house bunny remains very vigilant and will react instantly to an unfamiliar sound, smell or sudden movement. Learning about sensory capacities will help you to understand your rabbit's behaviour and the way in which she sees the world.

Charlie's alert ear carriage enables him to hear sounds from a variety of directions.

Hearing

Your rabbit has a very sharp sense of hearing; she can perk up her ears (unless she is floppy-eared) and move them in all directions. The large surface area allows the ears to pick up more sound waves than smaller ears can. This is why a bunny can hear the faintest noise from any direction and can identify its source immediately. In addition each ear can move independently of the other, enabling the bunny to listen in two directions at once.

Rabbits' ears are very sensitive to sound. If a bunny hears a loud or sudden noise she may bolt or flatten herself on the floor in a freezing posture. So it is best to avoid exposing your rabbit to loud noises (a blaring tv, noisy children, barking dogs, fireworks and so on).

Sight

The large eyes placed on the sides of the head offer the rabbit a panoramic view of approximately 360 degrees. A bunny can see all the way around and above her head, and notice a friend or foe approaching from any direction.

A rabbit's eyes are adapted for viewing objects at a distance, like those of other animals that depend on flight for survival. A sudden, faraway movement is quickly noticed by the rabbit. However, rabbits can't see well close-up because they have a blind spot in front of their noses. This is why your rabbit often runs between your feet and is unable to see a piece of food that's right in front of her nose.

Like other crepuscular animals, rabbits see better than us in dim light, probably having just black and white vision. When caring for a shy rabbit, or one who isn't in her usual surroundings, it is important to move slowly and quietly. Otherwise she could react by bolting and running into walls and furniture.

Smell

Rabbits have a very keen sense of smell and their nostrils are always twitching to sniff out the faintest odours. Their movement exposes the sensory pads which detect smells and transmit the information to the brain. The nose usually twitches at the rate of 20-120 times per minute but this may cease completely when a bunny is very relaxed. The twitching of the nostrils is complemented by the split upper lip. Its exposed moist surface behaves in a similar way to the wet nose of a dog, increasing the bunny's ability to detect odours.

Daisy with her namesakes.

Smell is a major form of communication among rabbits. Each animal produces special smells (pheromones) in the urine and from scent glands under the chin and tail.

Pheromones inform other rabbits about an individual's age, sex, social and reproductive status. When two rabbits are introduced for the first time they spend a lot of time sniffing each other to get to know one another and decide who is the more dominant. Through her sensitive nose a bunny can immediately detect the presence of an unfamiliar animal in her territory (such as a new rabbit or the neighbour's cat). Rabbits also identify people by their individual smell.

Having a sensitive nose, rabbits dislike the smell of strong cleaning agents, cigarettes, perfume and some foods. If a rabbit smells a heavy fragrance she may even attack the person wearing it. You should only use mild detergents (from the vet or pet shop) when cleaning your rabbit's possessions and environment.

Taste

The rabbit's tongue has about 8,000 taste buds, compared to 48,000 in the dog. This means that although rabbits can experience different tastes and develop definite food preferences, they don't necessarily recognise which plants are poisonous. When feeding twigs and wild plants, it is up to you to identify toxic varieties and keep them out of your bunny's reach.

Kellogg and Daisy love to chew on straw mats and carpet.

Touch

Rabbits use their whiskers and eyebrows to feel objects near the face and to find their way in the dark. Being as long as the body is wide, the whiskers help a bunny to judge her distance from an object (such as your furniture or a wall). The entire body surface is very sensitive to the touch, so stroking your rabbit when she is nervous or frightened will have a very soothing effect.

Body contact, such as the feeling of being in a burrow-like space (perhaps a tunnel or a cardboard box), and the presence of an animal friend are very reassuring for a rabbit. When you stroke your bunny, take care not to pull her whiskers or touch them unnecessarily.

chapter 11

Sexing and Neutering

Sexing

To determine the sex of your rabbit, lay the rabbit on its back and gently press the skin around the genital area. In male rabbits the penis will appear as a small rounded tip. Testicles are not fully formed in young males and may be withdrawn in cold weather.

Female rabbits have a small slit-like opening. Sexing a baby rabbit can be difficult and it is not unusual for people to make mistakes, particularly in pet shops. Your local shelter/breeder or an experienced rabbit vet will be able to confirm the sex of your bunny. This is particularly important if you are getting two or more rabbits.

Neutering

When rabbits become adolescent (from 10-12 weeks), they tend to become moody and very restless. They behave more aggressively towards other rabbits and people and also become less reliable as far as litter training is concerned. Both male and female bunnies may treat a family member of the opposite sex as a surrogate mate, circling and following that person and trying to mate with his or her arms or legs. In male bunnies, courtship behaviour often includes nipping the surrogate mate.

Neutering is one of the best things you can do for your rabbit. It will ease or eliminate these problems without changing your bunny's personality. Your pet will not realise that anything has changed and will become happier and more relaxed. Neutered bunnies are easier to litter train and their droppings and urine also become less smelly.

Female bunnies should be spayed when they are 5-6 months old while male bunnies can be neutered as soon as the testicles have descended, around 3-4 months of age. Spaying your female rabbit is very important because as many as 85% of adult females die of reproductive cancers if they are not neutered .

It is important to realise that the changes in behaviour associated with sexual maturity do not suddenly disappear - female rabbits may take a couple of months to generally calm down and male bunnies may go on spraying for a few months after being neutered. Not all aggressiveness is caused by hormonal changes: a rabbit who has become aggressive as a result of cruelty or mistreatment will not be cured by surgery but will need time and a lot of affection before he can trust his new carers.

Neutering is particularly important if you have more than one rabbit. It will, of course, prevent unwanted pregnancies and also make it possible for two rabbits to live happily together. A neutered pair can form a very strong relationship and often spend a lot of time grooming and huddling together. Two rabbits who are growing up together (including siblings) can suddenly become hostile and very aggressive towards each other. This results in serious fighting which can ruin the relationship permanently. Neutering or spaying can prevent this happening, provided it is done early enough. Neutering after the event may still be of some help but is generally no guarantee that their friendship will be restored.

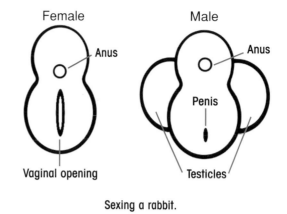

Sexing a rabbit.

Many facets of your bunny's sexuality will remain after neutering but in a gentler, more subdued form. The extent of sexual activity tends to reflect the rabbit's individual personality before neutering. Many neutered bunnies retain a certain amount of sexual interest and may continue some courting behaviour - a spayed female bunny is usually more tolerant of a male's advances than an unspayed one. Some bunnies lose all interest in sexual activity but their need for cuddles and affection, from humans as well as each other, remains the same.

Neutered rabbits need less food so make sure you adjust their diet slightly.

Caring for your newly-neutered bunny

When it is time to collect your bunny, make a note of when she was last fed - it is important that your bunny's digestive system doesn't shut down. Be sure to monitor urine and droppings in the first two days - if your bunny doesn't urinate or make any droppings during the first 24 hours let your vet know straight away.

When you bring your bunny home, she will need some time to recover - your bunny has been through surgery, has been housed in an unfamiliar cage and is probably feeling a bit uncomfortable after the operation. Keep her warm and in a quiet place and let her move around at her own pace - she knows what hurts and what doesn't.

Check your bunny twice a day to make sure that the genital area isn't too swollen (some swelling is normal) and that she hasn't pulled the stitches out. If the incision is very red, and possibly infected, take your bunny back to the vet. Remember to keep a newly spayed female away from male rabbits who may try to mate her and cause serious internal damage. Neutered males can still get a female rabbit pregnant up to three weeks after surgery. Most male rabbits begin to eat as soon as they get home, but females can take longer. If your rabbit hasn't eaten anything 24 hours after surgery, tempt her with all her favourite foods and, if necessary, syringe-feed her some baby food or blenderised rabbit mix (mix 1 part rabbit mix with two parts water).

chapter 12

Healthcare

Meeting your rabbit's needs for large and comfortable living quarters, a balanced diet, plenty of exercise, company and affection will help to keep your rabbit happy and healthy. A rabbit needs especially good care when she is very young or old, when she is under stress, when she is shedding her fur or when there's a sudden change in temperature. If you spend time with your rabbit every day and check her frequently you'll be quick to spot anything unusual in her appearance or behaviour. If you think there is something wrong, take your rabbit to the vet straight away - rabbits can deteriorate very quickly without expert veterinary care.

Signs that your rabbit is well		**Signs that your rabbit is ill**
Behaviour	Rabbit is active and lively, unless she's taking a nap. She keeps herself very clean.	Rabbit sits moping in a corner and doesn't show any interest in what is going on. In many cases she stops grooming.
Movement	Rabbit moves freely without limping.	Rabbit moves with difficulty or is unable to hop.
Appetite	Good, with bunny eating and drinking normally.	Rabbit is reluctant or unable to eat and drink.
Breathing	Quiet and regular (faster when your bunny is hot or afraid).	Rabbit is panting when she isn't hot or frightened and her nostrils are wide open.
Coat	Smooth and glossy. The fur feels soft and smells clean.	Dull and rough to the touch with bare patches or signs of parasites.
Skin	Clean, no signs of irritation, swellings or sores of any kind.	The usually loose skin is stretched tightly across your bunny's back.

Skin (continued)		Skin looks scaly, inflamed or lumpy. The rabbit scratches herself often.
Ears	React instantly to the slightest sound and are clean.	Little movement, folded back, smelly. Waxy or crusty deposits on the inside.
Eyes	Clear, bright and expressive.	Dull and staring. Teary discharge in the corners.
Nose	Twitching rhythmically, clean and dry.	Sneezing or snorting. Watery or thick, pus-like discharge.
Teeth	Straight, clean and of normal length.	Broken, overgrown or bent. The rabbit may be drooling.
Tummy	Completely clean and free from wounds or sores. Belly is roundish but not bloated and the sides are not caved in.	Caved in or hard, distended tummy. Fur dirty and encrusted with excreta. Tummy makes a lot of gurgling gas sounds.
Feet	Strong, clean feet.	Abscesses between the toes or sore hocks. Matted and dirty hair on the soles of the feet. Sticky fur on the inside of the front paws.
Claws	Of normal length.	Very long, torn at the ends.
Bottom	Clean and without sores.	Dirty and inflamed.
Droppings	Hard pellets are dry and well formed. Rabbit makes more or less the same amount of pellets every day.	Sticky and shapeless or much smaller and harder than usual. Bunny makes fewer or no droppings at all.

Urine	Rabbit urine can be clear, yellow, cloudy white, orange or red. This is usually normal and not a sign of illness.	Rabbit is straining when she needs to urinate. Orange, red or dense cloudy brown urine may be a sign that your bunny is unwell.
Weight	Stable.	Rabbit has put on or lost a lot of weight.

Examining your rabbit for health problems

It's important to do regular checks to make sure your bunny is healthy. If your rabbit is very tame and doesn't mind being handled you can do this on the floor but usually it is better to put your rabbit on a non-slippery surface such as on a towel which has been placed on a kitchen worktop.

Rabbits have a delicate skeletal structure and when a bunny kicks out suddenly with her back legs, the spinal cord can break or become dislocated in the weakest place (the lumbar vertebrae). For this reason it is important to hold your rabbit correctly during health checks.

The safest way to examine your bunny is to hold her facing away from you with her back resting against your chest. To do, this place both hands under your rabbit's chest and pick up your pet, holding her very close to your body. Now slide your left hand under the rabbit's forelegs and your right hand down her tummy, causing the back legs to stretch out to their full extent - this is very important to prevent your bunny from drawing up her back legs and

A change in behaviour may be the first sign of illness.

kicking out suddenly. A second person can now examine your bunny closely and look out for possible health problems.

What to look for

Look inside your rabbit's ears to see if there are any red or scaly patches. If the ears are dirty or smelly your rabbit could be ill. Make sure there is no discharge from the

Check that the teeth are clean, straight and of normal length.

An Elizabethan collar will prevent your rabbit nibbling at wounds or removing stitches.

nose or eyes. Carefully push back the lips to check that the teeth are straight, clean and of normal length. Look at your rabbit's chest and tummy for swellings, wounds and sores of any kind. Check that the bottom area isn't soiled or inflamed. Make sure the toenails are the right length and look at your rabbit's paws to see if they're dirty or sore. Check that the coat is in good condition and there are no bare patches in the fur. Push the fur backwards so you can see if the skin is scaly or inflamed.

When you put your rabbit back on the floor, give her a cuddle and maybe a little treat so she will not see this as an unpleasant experience. If you do regular health checks your rabbit will know what to expect and will not be nervous or afraid.

Important note: never leave your rabbit unattended when she is on a table or kitchen worktop because she may try to jump off. Make sure you have everything you need before you start examining your rabbit.

Looking after your rabbit patient

Bunnies are very quiet when they are not feeling well and they rarely whine or complain, even when in terrible pain. You will only see the suffering from the look in your rabbit's eyes and the changes in her behaviour and appearance. When nursing a sick bunny take note of the following points in order to make it easier for the vet to arrive at a diagnosis:

a) When did you first notice that your rabbit was ill?

b) What are the physical signs of the illness?

c) What are the changes in your rabbit's behaviour?

d) Has your bunny been eating and drinking normally? If so what, when and how much?

e) What are the droppings like? Is your rabbit constipated or does she have diarrhoea? It might be a good idea to take some stool samples along to your vet in case they need to be analysed.

When looking after your rabbit patient at home:

a) Follow the advice of your vet with regard to medication and diet.

b) Keep your bunny warm and dry and protect her from drafts and changes in temperature.

c) Keep your bunny in quiet stress-free surroundings and avoid any loud noise or activity which might disturb or worry her.

d) Don't be upset if your rabbit bites you: she is probably confused and in pain and needs your sympathy and understanding more than anything now. Keep your rabbit company and cuddle her often.

e) If your bunny has an infectious illness, keep her bed very clean and change the bedding and litter frequently. Your vet will be able to recommend a safe disinfectant.

f) If your rabbit is bonded to another rabbit they should be kept together, even if the first rabbit has a contagious illness. The second rabbit has probably already been exposed to it and separating them will be very stressful for both of them.

g) If your rabbit's condition deteriorates, do not wait: take your rabbit to the vet without delay.

Finding a good rabbit vet

It is important to look for a vet before your bunny gets ill. If you know other rabbit carers ask them if they can recommend a good vet. Alternatively look in the Yellow Pages for surgeries which specialise in small animals or exotic pets.

It's a good idea to have a few questions ready to help you decide if a vet is interested in or familiar with rabbit medicine. For example:

• Does the vet see many rabbit patients?

• Does the vet recommend neutering rabbits? (Yes, to improve health and behaviour.)

- How many rabbits has the vet neutered or spayed in the last 12 months?
- What was the success rate? 90% is too low, hopefully 98-100%.
- Has the vet done any other operations on rabbits?
- Does the vet want the rabbit to fast before surgery? (Rabbits should not fast before an operation and, because they cannot vomit, there is no danger that they will inhale vomit during surgery.)
- Will your bunny be given a thorough health check before the operation?
- What anaesthetics does the vet use? Isofluorane is the safest to use on rabbits.
- How will the vet and nurses care for your rabbit after the operation (oxygen, warmth, stimulation)? How often will they be checking how your bunny is doing? Will your bunny be housed next to noisy cats and dogs?
- What antibiotics are dangerous for rabbits? (lincomycin, clindamycin, amoxicillin and most of the "-cillin" drugs, like penicillin).
- Should a rabbit be vaccinated? (Yes, against VHD and Myxomatosis.)
- What is the best way of preventing hairballs? Give your rabbit hay (this should always be available), plenty of exercise and brush her coat regularly (every day during moulting).

Don't be shy about asking these questions - after all you are considering employing somebody to do a job for you. You may need to make several telephone calls before you get the "right" answers. When you do, take your bunny to the vet for a check-up - this should give you a good idea of whether you've made the right choice.

Getting there
Pick up your rabbit carefully and put her in her travel cage - a strong cardboard box can also be used provided the lid is secure and there are holes in the sides for ventilation. Line the carrier with newspaper and hay or straw. Drive smoothly to prevent your bunny from sliding around in her carrier.

Giving medication to your bunny
You will need patience and a little practice if you have to give your bunny medication. Ask your vet to show you what to do and, if possible, get somebody to help you at home. Always read the label and follow the instructions carefully - if you're not sure about something check with your vet first. Giving your bunny medication will be much easier if you have her on a non-slippery surface. Make sure your hands are very clean and that you have everything you need before you start.

Applying a cream or ointment
Clean the wound using a sterile pad and trim the fur if necessary. Apply the ointment or cream from the centre of the wound to the outside to avoid carrying germs from the

fur to the centre of the wound. Be careful not to apply too much medication or your bunny might lick it off and ingest it during grooming.

Oral medication

You can give your bunny tea or liquid medications using a dropper or a plastic syringe (without the needle). Gently hold your bunny's ears flat against the back to stop your rabbit wriggling. Pull down the lip on one side and place the syringe in the corner of the mouth behind the front teeth. Push the plunger of the syringe down slowly so your rabbit doesn't choke on the liquid. Don't let go of your bunny until she has swallowed the medicine.

To give your bunny a capsule or tablet, gently pull the lips apart with your thumb and forefinger. Place the capsule or pill as far as possible to the back of the mouth - your bunny should then readily swallow. A pill popper (from a pet shop) can also be used.

P.S. Medication can also be added to your bunny's food or water. However, this makes it difficult to assess whether the medicine has actually been taken since most rabbits tend to avoid medicated food and will also drink much less if they don't like the taste of the water. I use Seven Cereal baby food to disguise medicines - rabbits like it because it is sweet, but be careful your rabbit doesn't become addicted to it or she may then refuse normal food. You could also try putting some medication in a cabbage leaf or a slice of banana.

Eye medication

It's a good idea to ask someone to hold your rabbit when you have to give her eye medication. Gently lift the upper lid or pull down the lower lid and insert the drops, taking care not to touch the surface of the eye with the tip of the applicator. Alternatively, apply an ointment line along the length of the eyelid and when the lids close the medication will be distributed evenly over the entire surface of the eye.

Ear medication

Check that your rabbit's ears are clean and, if necessary, remove any waxy or crusty deposits using a cotton bud dipped in olive or mineral oil. To apply ointment or drops, hold the ear upright and insert the applicator tip or dropper. The rabbit's ear canal descends vertically and then slightly turns toward the inside. The place of the infection is usually deep inside the ear at the deviation of the canal. In order to be effective medications must reach this part of the ear. However, pushing the applicator tip too far down could do a lot of damage to the rabbit's delicate middle ear structure. The safest thing to do is to keep your bunny's ear upright and massage it for a few seconds to distribute the medication to the bottom of the ear canal.

Illnesses

These are some of the more common illnesses and health problems rabbits may suffer from, with some advice on what to do. If in doubt, always consult a vet.

Abscesses

Abscesses are swellings which can form in the skin as well as in internal organs. They are often caused by bacteria and other organisms infecting a scratch, cut or sore (as a result of two rabbits fighting, for example). Abscesses can also form in the rabbit's mouth following a broken tooth or gum infection. If you suspect your rabbit has an abscess, take her to the vet immediately.

Bloat

If your rabbit's stomach is swollen and hard and your bunny is short of breath, she may have bloat. This can happen when a rabbit eats too much green food such as clover and wet grass. It can also be caused by mouldy hay, spoiled food or irregular feeding. Rabbits have a very sensitive bacterial flora in the intestine and an incorrect diet can cause the wrong kind of bacteria to multiply, resulting in excess gas production and a swollen, distended belly.

Other symptoms include restlessness, loud grinding of the teeth, persistent drumming of the back feet and shortness of breath (because the stomach is pressing against the lungs). Sometimes the sick bunny just sits hunched up in a corner with eyes glazed and staring into space.

Bloat can be fatal so get your rabbit to the vet as soon as possible.

Cancers - Reproductive

By far the most common type of cancer in rabbits is uterine cancer which affects the glands in the wall of the womb. Up to 85% of unspayed female rabbits develop uterine cancer by the time they are 4 or 5 years old, and this is usually fatal. Luckily you can prevent uterine and other reproductive cancers by having your rabbit spayed.

Coccidiosis

Coccidiosis is a very serious disease which can affect the intestine (intestinal coccidiosis) or the liver (hepatic coccidiosis). It is caused by microscopic parasites which live in the lining of the intestine or, in the case of hepatic coccidiosis, in the lining of the bile ducts and liver. These organisms multiply very quickly and are passed out with the rabbit's droppings. They contaminate the food, water and bedding and can easily be transmitted to other rabbits, so keep any sick bunny isolated. A rabbit becomes infected again when she ingests her droppings or licks her soiled fur during grooming. Young bunnies are particularly at risk.

Symptoms include a rough coat, persistent diarrhoea, rapid weight loss and a bloated tummy. The rabbit looks very weak and often sits trembling and grinding her teeth loudly in pain.

Coccidiosis is very often fatal. Even if the rabbit survives, the lining of the intestine may be permanently damaged, preventing the normal absorption of food nutrients. If detected at an early stage, coccidiosis can be treated successfully with sulphur-based drugs, so seek professional help immediately. Remember to take a stool sample to the vet for analysis.

Disinfect your bunny's living quarters thoroughly and replace contaminated food, water and bedding as often as possible. In some countries medicated rabbit food containing a drug called coccidiostat is available commercially.

Constipation

If your rabbit stops eating and produces virtually no droppings, she probably has constipation. A constipated bunny sits hunched up in a corner, sometimes with a bloated belly. This usually happens when a rabbit doesn't eat enough vegetables and fibre.

If you think your rabbit may be constipated, take her to the vet without delay. Also, remove the dry food and offer some hay and fresh foods. Make sure she has plenty of fresh water (this should always be available) and gets enough exercise.

Cuts and wounds

Trim the fur around the injury and clean minor cuts and wounds using an antiseptic solution (available from the vet). Alternatively, dissolve some salt in warm water (boiled and allowed to cool) and bathe the wound gently with cotton wool. Take your bunny to the vet if the area becomes red and inflamed as this may result in an abscess.

If your rabbit is bleeding, apply pressure to the wound and bandage it until your vet is able to see it - ice and styptic pencil can also be used to reduce on-going blood loss. Eye scratches and injuries are particularly serious and require immediate veterinary attention to avoid loss of sight.

Prevent injuries by watching your rabbit during introductions and when she is outdoors.

Diarrhoea

Diarrhoea isn't a disease in itself, more a sign that something else is wrong in the body. It can be the result of your rabbit eating certain food or can also be caused by stress, infection of the stomach and the intestine, damp bedding, cold and drafts. The wrong type of antibiotics can cause diarrhoea and even kill your rabbit.

If your bunny has diarrhoea:

- Wipe or wash her bottom with warm soapy water, rinse and dry well.
- Keep your rabbit warm.
- Change the litter and bedding frequently.
- Don't feed high-protein foods such as rabbit mix and treats; make sure your rabbit has plenty of hay, straw and fresh drinking water.
- Raspberry, strawberry and bramble leaves will help relieve diarrhoea because of their astringent properties.

A little live natural yoghurt will help revitalise the lining of the stomach and intestine. Probiotics can also be used to promote the friendly bacteria and eliminate the harmful ones. If diarrhoea continues for longer than a couple of hours get your bunny to the vet immediately (take a stool sample along for analysis).

Electric shocks

If your bunny has nibbled through an electric cable and is lying unconscious or semi-conscious, call in your vet immediately. While you're waiting, keep your bunny warm and cover her with a towel or blanket.

It is very important to keep all electric cables out of reach or your bunny will try to nibble at them sooner or later.

Enteritis

Enteritis is a very serious disease which affects mainly young rabbits (between four and eight weeks old). It may have a variety of causes, such as bacterial infection, but the most common factor is usually a high-energy, low-fibre diet. Enteritis often happens when a young bunny changes quickly from a milk-based to a dry food diet. Dry food is high in energy and protein content but relatively low in fibre, leading to changes in the pH and bacterial flora of the intestine.

Typical symptoms include jelly-like diarrhoea, a soiled underside, bloated tummy, teeth-crunching and excessive drinking (to combat dehydration). Once a rabbit has enteritis she can die very quickly (usually within 24 hours) so early veterinary care is essential. Always make changes in the diet very gradually to prevent digestive upsets. Offer your rabbit plenty of hay and fresh drinking water. Minimise stress and keep the living area scrupulously clean.

Fly strike

Fly infestation is a very serious problem, especially in the summer, and is often fatal. It occurs when flies lay their eggs in open wounds or faeces-soiled fur. The maggots hatch very quickly (within 12 to 24 hours) and immediately start eating into the rabbit's flesh. Infested rabbits sit crouching in a corner, usually in a state of shock.

Your bunny is particularly at risk during hot weather (fly season) and if she makes soft unformed droppings (usually as a result of a diet too rich in treats and dried food). Prevention is vital so feed your rabbit a balanced diet and check her bottom twice a day for signs of infestation.

If your bunny has fly strike use a flea comb and tweezers to remove the eggs and maggots (including those which may have entered the vaginal and anal openings). Spot-cleaning your rabbit with chlorahexadine solution is better than bathing as flies are attracted to moist places. If you do wet your rabbit, make sure you dry her thoroughly with a towel and hairdryer on a low heat setting. It's a good idea to clip or shave the fur around the affected area to prevent further infestation. Maggots cause a great deal of tissue damage so it is vital to take your rabbit to the vet for a check-up and injections.

Fractures

The two most common areas of fracture are those of the spine and the legs. They are usually the result of a rabbit falling from a high place, being accidentally stepped on or being caught in a closing door. A rabbit can break her spine during energetic play or when she's not being held properly and kicks out suddenly with her back legs. For this reason, it is important to discourage children and hesitant, inexperienced adults from handling your rabbit. If a fracture occurs, seek veterinary care immediately.

Hairballs

When rabbits groom themselves it is natural for them to swallow some hair; this is usually expelled with the droppings, making them stick together. Long-haired rabbits and those who are moulting should be groomed regularly to prevent hairballs. Blockages are more likely to form if the rabbit is fed a diet which is too high in protein and calories, thus slowing down her digestive system. Offering your rabbit plenty of high fibre foods like hay, straw, twigs, seagrass mats and fresh foods will keep the digestive tract moving at the correct rate and help the rabbit to expel the likes of hair and carpet fibres in the droppings.

Blockages are very serious in rabbits because they cannot vomit and the opening from their stomach to their intestine is quite small. Signs include loss of appetite, smaller, harder or no droppings. However, the rabbit is often lively and bright so the condition may go unnoticed until it's too late.

If your rabbit is prone to hairballs, offer her plenty of fresh foods, hay and water. Make sure she gets plenty of exercise and brush her regularly (every day during the shedding season) to remove the dead fur. If your rabbit doesn't start eating within a few hours, take her to the vet.

Heat exhaustion

Heat exhaustion is often the result of a rabbit being left in hot, direct sunlight for a long time, for example in a sunny, poorly-ventilated room. It can also happen when travelling with your bunny in a very hot car. Symptoms include breathing very rapidly with the nostrils and mouth open, trembling and lying down fully stretched.

If your rabbit is suffering from heat stroke, put her in the shade or a cool place at once. Offer her water at room temperature and some fresh, crisp greens. Apply a cool (not ice cold) wet flannel first to her forehead, then to the back and legs until she begins to breathe normally. Heat stroke may be fatal so prevention is very important. Always shelter your rabbit from direct sunlight and other sources of heat (such as radiators, fires, electric heaters and so on).

Large dewlap

A well-developed dewlap (roll of skin under the chin) is more common in older female bunnies of medium and large breeds - smaller breeds usually maintain their neat build throughout life. A large dewlap sometimes makes it difficult for a bunny to keep her bottom area clean. The skin in the deep fold can also become moist and inflamed.

To prevent a large dewlap forming, feed your bunny a balanced diet so she doesn't become overweight. Vets can surgically reduce the dewlap if it causes problems and discomfort, even when the rabbit's weight is normal. However, be careful the rabbit doesn't put the weight back on after the operation or the skin may stretch again.

Myxomatosis

Myxomatosis is a very serious disease that can be transmitted by insects (usually mosquitoes and rabbit fleas) or other rabbits, for example when wild rabbits come into contact with your bunny while she is in the garden. Within a few days of becoming infected the rabbit develops painful swellings on the eyelids, nose, lips, ears and in the genital area. Shortly afterwards the swellings break open and the pus-like discharge, which sticks to food and bedding, causes further infection. Later, swellings appear all over the body, the rabbit loses appetite, has difficulty breathing, and develops a very high temperature. Myxomatosis is usually fatal.

The best form of protection is to vaccinate your rabbit once a year (twice yearly in high-risk areas). Vaccination is best done at the beginning of summer (May - June).

Obesity

Rabbits will become overweight if they are fed too much and don't get enough exercise. Some rabbits eat out of boredom if they are confined to a cage for most of the time. Others seem to be constantly hungry so it is easy to overfeed them, especially when they beg for food. Overweight bunnies find it difficult to hop around

Bored or lazy bunnies are more prone to becoming overweight.

Dark toenails require careful trimming in order to avoid cutting into the quick.

and be active as this requires too much effort. They also tend to have a bigger dewlap and tummy so find it harder to keep themselves clean

To keep your bunny healthy and lively, make sure she gets plenty of exercise and eats the right kind of food. If your bunny needs to lose weight you should reduce her intake of high calorie foods like rabbit mix and fruit. See the chapter on Feeding.

Overgrown claws

Wild rabbits keep their claws worn down naturally by burrowing. However your house rabbit will probably need to have her nails clipped regularly, especially if she doesn't get much opportunity to dig or hop on hard surfaces (like concrete or patio stones). The nails then grow too long, curling inwards and interfering with movement.

To trim the toenails use a pair of pet nailclippers. Place the rabbit on a table or in your lap and hold each paw in turn, pushing the fur back a little. The front paws have five toes (one of them on the side of the leg), the back paws four. In light-coloured nails it is easy to see the central (live) part of the nail, where the nerves and blood vessels are. If your bunny has dark toenails, hold each paw to the light or ask somebody to shine a torch underneath the nail to be clipped. This will make it easier to see which part of the nail is live. Only clip a little bit off, cutting straight across to prevent splintering. Be careful not to cut into the quick because this hurts and may cause bleeding. If this happens use a styptic pencil to stem the flow of blood or bathe your bunny's foot in a mild antiseptic solution.

Parasites - external

If your rabbit looks uncomfortable and keeps scratching herself she may be infested with parasites. External parasites spread by direct contact and include fleas, lice, ticks and mites.

Ear mites

Your bunny's ears (especially floppy ears) are an ideal hiding place for microscopic parasites (mites) which burrow into the skin causing intense irritation. This condition is also known as ear mange or canker and typical symptoms include red patches and sores, followed by the appearance of brownish crusts inside the rabbit's ears. The affected bunny shakes her head very frequently, as if trying to get rid of the parasites. She also holds the head to one side and paws repeatedly at her ears, doing herself more damage and causing the mange to spread.

Do not try to remove the deposits by scraping them away as this may cause bleeding and is very painful for your bunny - some of the pieces are also likely to fall deeper into the ear canal. Use olive or mineral oil to soften the crusts and later wipe the inside of your bunny's ears gently with some cotton wool. Repeat every 2-3 days for a few weeks until the ear canal is clean and healed. Take your rabbit to the vet for an injection or a special cream/ointment to treat mites.

Mites can be very persistent and live off their host for several weeks so keep your rabbit's living quarters very clean and change the bedding every day. Do not use old, dusty hay or straw for bedding as this is where the mites may have come from in the first place. Ear mites are highly contagious.

Fleas

Fleas are skin parasites which usually affect wild rabbits but, from time to time, infest domestic bunnies as well. Rabbits may get fleas from other pets, for example cats.

Fleas are mahogany in colour and between 1.5-5 mm long; they wriggle or jump and tend to gather on the head, neck, back and the base of the ears. The small dark specks are not flea eggs but droppings. The affected bunny scratches herself very frequently, shaking and tilting her head and the skin soon becomes red and visibly irritated.

Fleas feed on the blood of their host and reproduce by laying eggs in all sorts of places such as on the ground, in bedding (human or pet), furniture, carpets, on the floor and in any crack or crevice that's available. Eggs can easily be carried from the garden into the house by a pet or on your shoes. Within a few days (2-12 in summer, longer in winter) the larvae emerge and the life cycle begins again. Fleas are not only external pests but can also transmit specific disorders like tapeworm and, of course, myxomatosis. Rabbit fleas also bite humans.

To solve the problem of flea infestation you will need to treat your garden and house as well as your rabbit. If fleas are inside the house, vacuum-cleaning can be very effective in sucking the eggs out of the carpet - don't forget to hoover in those hard-to-reach places and also the cushions, settees and so on. Vacuuming under the furniture is particularly important if your house bunny likes to spend time under a bed or couch.

A mixture of boiling water and ammonia can be used on any concrete floor to kill both fleas and eggs. Alternatively, you can get sprays and various other products for indoor and outdoor use from pet shops as well as garden centres. Before using these products, make sure you check with the vet. Cat and kitten flea powder can be used successfully on rabbits or ask your vet for advice.

Fur mites

Fur mites are usually found around the rabbit's head, shoulders and back but can exist away from the animal host too. Typical signs include bare patches in the fur, red flaky skin and crusty deposits. Many rabbits do not find fur mites irritating and barely scratch as a result. Fur mites are highly contagious and can be passed to and from other household pets, including cats and dogs. They can also be transmitted to humans, causing a form of short-term dermatitis.

If you suspect that your bunny may be suffering from fur mites you should handle her carefully using gloves and disinfect her living quarters thoroughly. Replace infected bedding and litter.

Cat flea powder can be used to treat fur mites but several applications will be necessary. Alternatively, take your rabbit to the vet for treatment.

Lice

Lice also feed on the blood of rabbits causing discomfort and irritation. Unlike fleas however, they live the whole of their life cycle on the animal host, laying their eggs or nits in the fur. The eggs are white and secured to the coat by a natural adhesive; they are easy to see in dark-coloured rabbits, but will be noticed in any fur during grooming.

To treat lice infestation ask your vet to prescribe an appropriate insecticide for use on your bunny. Repeat the treatment several times in order to eliminate the succeeding generations of lice emerging from the nits. Lice are not very common and keeping your bunny in clean surroundings will help to prevent infestation.

Ticks

These parasites occasionally infest rabbits, feeding on their blood for several days. When they are full they drop off naturally. Ticks can be removed by cutting off their air supply with a smear of vaseline and then detaching them with tweezers. Be sure to remove the head part of the tick at the same time to prevent infection.

Parasites - internal

If a bunny is eating well but is not in good condition she may have worms. These are sometimes visible in the droppings and can be treated using a puppy wormer. Consult your veterinarian and follow the dosage instructions carefully - especially if your rabbit is very young.

Pin worms

You don't usually see signs of pin worm infestation unless this is very severe. Typical symptoms include slow growth rate, poor condition, rough fur and little resistance to other intestinal diseases. To avoid infestation keep your bunny's home very clean and use a mild puppy wormer (available from the vet).

Tapeworms

Rabbits act as the intermediate host in the life cycle of both dog and cat tapeworms. Infected cats and dogs produce segments of the tapeworm in their faeces; these segments containing eggs may then be ingested together with green food by a browsing rabbit. Inside the bunny, tapeworm eggs develop into larvae within a liquid-filled cyst, creating a large swelling. House bunnies grazing in a garden shared with a dog or cat can certainly develop larval cysts, for instance under the skin, in the abdominal region or in the liver.

Make sure your cat or dog is regularly wormed and doesn't defecate on the lawn in areas your bunny has access to. Always wash all green food and vegetables thoroughly before feeding them to your rabbit. If a cyst does occur, the vet may be able to remove it. Tapeworms do not usually cause the death of a rabbit unless they are present in very large numbers.

Pasteurella

Pasteurellosis is a bacterial disease caused by the organism *Pasteurella Multocida*. It is estimated that as many as 85% of rabbits carry the organism in their nasal passages naturally but, given certain stress factors, the condition can progress and lead to more serious health problems, for example snuffles (the most common manifestation), pneumonia, runny eyes, abscesses, inner and middle ear infections, septicaemia, and so on.

Typical signs include persistent sneezing and a runny nose. The rabbit uses her forepaws to wipe away the white/yellowish discharge and relieve the irritation with the result that the fur on the inside of the forelegs appears wet and matted. The mucous membranes of the nose become swollen and inflamed and the rabbit generally looks poorly. As the illness progresses the lungs may also become infected, making breathing very difficult, leading to pneumonia or even death.

Snuffles is highly infectious. If caught in the early stages, this condition can be treated with antibiotics. However, these only have a temporary effect (if any at all) on the bacteria responsible, preventing the illness from getting worse rather than offering a complete cure. Seek veterinary help immediately. Vitamin C in the water can also help. The best form of prevention is to keep your rabbit in dry, comfortable, stress-free and well-ventilated surroundings. Avoid draughts and changes in temperature and feed your bunny a balanced diet. Empty litter trays regularly. Use a vapouriser (available from the chemist) to help your bunny breathe more easily.

Pneumonia

Damp bedding and dirty living quarters can predispose a bunny to pneumonia (inflammation of the lungs). Pneumonia may be caused by bacterial or viral infection and is more likely to happen during times of stress. It can become a chronic condition and even lead to the bunny's death. It often represents the final stage of snuffles.

Signs of pneumonia include a high body temperature, rough coat, loss of appetite and, usually, a discharge from the nose. The rabbit tends to sit huddled in a corner and finds it very difficult to breathe because her lungs are filled with fluid. She may hold her head back and her tongue, lips and ears turn a bluish colour. It is important to take your bunny to the vet without delay. Antibiotics can help treat pneumonia, provided the condition is recognised early. Take care to avoid drafts and sudden changes in temperature. Keeping your rabbit in clean, stress-free, well-ventilated surroundings will reduce the chances of your bunny getting ill in the first place.

Red Urine

Red urine which doesn't contain blood clots is due to the incomplete metabolism of certain food nutrients and is not a sign of illness. It may happen when your bunny eats beetroot or other fresh foods.

The presence of blood in the urine (to be confirmed by a urine analysis) requires immediate veterinary attention.

Ringworm

Contrary to what its name would suggest, ringworm isn't a parasitic organism but a fungus. Ringworm causes loss of fur in circular patches. The skin becomes itchy, scaly and inflamed. Ringworm usually affects the feet and legs of young rabbits but can be seen in adult rabbits in any part of the body. It produces similar symptoms in humans, for instance on the arms and legs, so you should handle the affected rabbit carefully using gloves.

Take your bunny to the vet for treatment and ask for a safe disinfectant to use in the rabbit's environment. Ringworm spores can survive for a long time so keeping your bunny's home and accessories very clean will help to stop the problem reccurring.

Runny eyes

Eye infections can have very common causes, such as dusty hay, dirt, drafts, cold, scratches inflicted during fighting, urine sprayed by another rabbit, ingrowing eyelashes and long woolly hair (in Angoras). Dirty bedding containing excess ammonia (from the urine) can also irritate the eyes. Weepy eyes can be the result of overgrown teeth and respiratory infections.

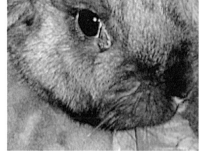

Wipe the eye from the inner to the outer corner using some cotton wool and warm salted water (boiled and allowed to cool). This will prevent build-up of the discharge and damage to the delicate skin around the eyes. Use a new piece of cotton wool for each eye. Your vet will be able to prescribe some medication.

Runny eyes can have a variety of causes.

Runny nose and sneezing

This can also be an allergic reaction to stale, dusty bedding and the use of very strong cleaners and disinfectants around your bunny's home. To avoid these symptoms make sure you only use fresh hay and straw and mild cleaning products which don't give out irritating fumes.

Do not confuse occasional sneezing with a more serious contagious illness called snuffles (see Pasteurella). If in doubt, take your bunny to the vet immediately.

Sore hocks

You should inspect the soles of your rabbit's feet regularly for signs of injury or build-up of dirt between the toes, which can be a source of irritation and infection. Ulcers and open sores

Rabbits can also develop sore hocks when they live on carpeted floors.

sometimes appear on the bottom surface of the back feet and later abscesses may develop. In some cases all four paws are affected.

A rabbit with sore hocks tries to shift her weight from one back foot to the other, looking restless and very uncomfortable. She may avoid hopping around, lose her appetite and generally look unwell - some rabbits even die if the infection spreads to other parts of the body through the bloodstream.

The following factors can contribute to sore hocks:

a) body weight - if a rabbit is heavy this puts more pressure on the surface of the feet.

b) if the foot pad area is relatively small compared to the size of the body.

c) if the rabbit has very delicate skin under the paws.

d) if the rabbit was born with only a thin layer of fur on the soles of the feet.

e) if the fur pad has been trimmed away during grooming.

f) if the hair under the paws is matted and soiled.

g) if the toenails need cutting.

h) if the floor surface of the pen or the carpet is too rough on your bunny's feet.

i) if the bedding is dirty and damp.

j) if bunny has constantly wet feet because of a dripping water bottle or a spilt water bowl.

You should treat sore hocks carefully using some antiseptic ointment from the vet. Bandaging the feet can also help the healing process. In severe cases, antibiotic treatment is needed to combat the infection. Relapses are usually frequent. Keep your rabbit on clean, dry, and soft bedding - synthetic sheepskin rugs are ideal.

If the furry pads are dirty and matted, gently bathe your bunny in mild soapy water rather than clipping the fur in this delicate area. Avoid using pens with a wire mesh floor or provide a synthetic sheepskin rug, towel or a flat board to sit on.

Teeth

Overgrown Incisors

A rabbit's front teeth (incisors) can grow 1cm or more a month. Because of this unique characteristic, it is essential that the upper pair of incisors meet the lower pair at the correct angle to wear each other down during chewing. If a rabbit's lower jaw is longer than the upper jaw, the two pairs of incisors are slightly out of line and no longer grind together (malocclusion). In such cases the teeth will continue to grow until the bunny is unable to eat properly.

Malocclusion can be inherited or the result of an unbalanced diet. Make sure the rabbit eats all parts of the rabbit mix (including the pellets) and doesn't just pick out her favourite bits. The pellets are usually where the vitamins and minerals (including calcium) are found. A diet deficient in calcium and vitamin D is very likely to cause dental and skeletal problems later on. For this reason, it is also a good idea to let the rabbit spend some time in the garden whenever possible, since direct sunlight produces vitamin D which is essential for the absorption of calcium.

Occasionally a rabbit breaks off one or both upper or lower incisors. The opposite tooth will then grow longer because it doesn't have anything to rub against. If the tooth bed has been traumatised during the incident there is also a chance that the incisor(s) might "turn" slightly and grow at an abnormal angle, causing a permanent form of malocclusion.

Overgrown upper incisors usually curve sharply inwards and grow back into the upper jaw. Lower front teeth grow into a broader curve outside the rabbit's mouth and may become embedded in the nostril area if no action is taken. Malocclusion can also cause painful abscesses.

Overgrown incisors must be clipped every 4-6 weeks - ideally under sedation or anaesthesia. Trimming the teeth yourself may result in a tooth breaking and the gum becoming infected. To prevent overgrown teeth, give your bunny plenty of hard food to nibble at, such as carrots and broccoli stems. A branch of apple tree with the bark left on is ideal to keep your bunny's teeth worn down. You can also buy gnawing blocks and mineral/vitamin licks your bunny can nibble at from most pet shops. Giving your pet a fruit tree branch or other gnawing material will not prevent or correct malocclusion but will help your bunny keep her front teeth short if they meet correctly.

Recently, vets have started to remove overgrown incisors to avoid constant clipping. One of my rabbits, Sweetpea, is doing very well after this type of operation. He can eat dry mix and chopped vegetables and fruit and now his teeth do not get in the way when he eats. He even eats small willow twigs, hay and parsley stalks by sucking them into his mouth like spaghetti.

Overgrown Molars

Your bunny's back teeth (molars) also grow continuously, although much

Watermelon may be enjoyable but be sure to also provide your rabbit with plenty of hard food to nibble at.

89

more slowly than the incisors. Overgrown molars form spurs which produce soreness and ulceration on the tongue and the inside of the cheeks, and later abscesses may develop.

Overgrown molars will cause a bunny to dribble because she cannot keep her mouth closed (look out for signs); if the hair on the face and under the chin is constantly wet with saliva, the rabbit is also likely to develop moist dermatitis. The rabbit gradually stops eating as this becomes very painful, so weight loss will be obvious. Overgrown molars must be trimmed by the vet under anaesthetic. To prevent overgrown molars, make sure the bunny has a balanced diet and eats plenty of grass, straw and hay.

Urine burn

Urine burn may be a symptom of something more serious, so it is important the vet sees your rabbit as soon as possible. Urine that dries on your bunny's delicate skin around the genitals and the inside of the back legs can cause severe irritation. Bathe the affected area gently but thoroughly in soapy or salted water; rinse and dry well. Apply an antiseptic soothing cream or an antibiotic ointment from the vet. Prevent urine scalding by offering your rabbit absorbent litter and by keeping her living area clean. Overweight rabbits and those with a large dewlap will find it more difficult to keep themselves clean, so gradually change their diet or ask your vet for advice.

Viral Haemorrhagic Disease (VHD)

VHD first appeared in Britain in 1992 and has since spread very rapidly across the country. It affects both wild rabbits and domestic rabbits but cannot be transmitted to humans or other animals.

There are many ways in which the virus can be spread, for example:

- Through direct contact with other rabbits (these may be carriers of the disease without showing any of the symptoms).
- If your rabbit has water or food (such as wild plants or grass) contaminated by infected wild rabbits.
- Birds may bring the virus on their feet or in their droppings, which your bunny could eat when she grazes in the garden.
- Mice and rats could pass on the virus if they come near your rabbit.
- You or your cat or dog could accidentally spread the virus by stepping on contaminated (wild) rabbit droppings.
- It may be blown on the wind or transmitted by insects such as flies.
- You could pick up the virus from other people's rabbits or if another person handles your rabbit (humans can carry the virus on their skin and clothes).

Very young bunnies (under 8 weeks old) rarely get ill but older rabbits usually die from VHD within a short space of time (1-3 days at the most). They may die suddenly without showing any sign of disease or they may become very ill, have difficulty breathing, go off their food, have a high temperature and bleed from the nose and bottom.

A sick bunny may look very poorly and often just lies down, showing no interest in what is going on; some rabbits have spasms and cry or scream before dying. Others get only a mild form of the disease and then get better.

The easiest form of prevention is to have your rabbit vaccinated - a single injection will protect your bunny for up to 12 months and is safe for use on young rabbits too.

Wry neck

Wry neck may be the result of cerebral infection or infection of the inner or middle ear. It is sometimes associated with infections of the upper respiratory system.

The affected rabbit holds her head to one side and finds it difficult to keep her balance. She may be unable to stand or walk in a straight line and usually goes round in circles. In the later stages she loses her appetite and may stop eating altogether. Seek veterinary care immediately.

Helpful items to include in a Bunny First Aid Kit:
- Scissors
- Nail clippers
- Sterile gauze pads
- Adhesive tape
- Antiseptic solution for use on wounds and scratches
- Styptic pencil (available from the chemist) to reduce on-going blood loss
- Cotton wool pads
- Ear buds
- A plastic syringe or medicine dropper
- Mineral oil to treat ear mite infestation (olive oil can also be used)
- Mild medicated shampoo
- Salt to disinfect wounds or bathe your rabbit
- A safe disinfectant for use on feeding utensils and around the home
- Flannel; a wet flannel on your bunny's back will help keep her cool on very hot days
- A factsheet with your rabbit's medical notes and special needs
- Your vet's name, address and phone number

Giving your rabbit a bath

Bathing a rabbit can be very stressful and should be avoided if possible. The majority of rabbits keep themselves very clean but sick, overweight or disabled bunnies may need to be bathed from time to time. If your rabbit doesn't keep her bottom area very clean, clip the hair very short around the genitals and the inside of the back legs to prevent the fur matting and to make cleaning easier.

I find that the kitchen sink is ideal to bath a rabbit. Fill it with warm water and make sure you have everything ready before you start: shampoo or salt for a saline bath, towels, hairdryer and maybe a shower attachment for rinsing. Lower your bunny gently into the water and talk to her soothingly so she doesn't feel nervous. If you have your rabbit facing away from you she'll be less likely to jump out of the water. Never leave your bunny on her own while she is in the sink because it only takes a few seconds for an accident to happen.

If your rabbit is having a bottom bath there's no need to get her chest and front legs wet; just let your bunny rest her forelegs on the edge of the sink or in your hand so she feels safer. Wash the fur gently using a mild shampoo; if the bottom area is very dirty you may need to let your bunny soak for a few minutes. Rinse your rabbit well and dab the fur using a soft towel. One of my rabbit likes jumping out of the sink onto the draining board at the end of each bath so I always cover the surface with a large towel (rabbits don't like slippery surfaces).

If it's a hot sunny day you can let your rabbit dry in the garden, otherwise you will need to use a hairdryer. Make sure the setting isn't too high (feel the warm air with your hand) and keep the cable out of the way or your bunny may try to nibble at it. My rabbit prefers to dry by her favourite radiator in the sitting room. I put a big fluffy towel at the foot of the radiator and make sure the room is warm and draught-free. I usually bath my rabbit in the evening and leave the heating on overnight.

Never leave a rabbit unattended in the bath or sink.

My rabbit's care sheet

(Rabbit's photo)

Carer's name:

Address:

Phone number:

Vet's name:

Address:

Phone number:

Surgery hours:

Medical notes:

Rabbit's name:

Date of birth:

Breed:

Colour/Description:

Sex: Weight:

Feeding notes:

Favourite foods:

Vaccinations:

Favourite activity:

Neutered:

Litter trained:

Insurance Details:

Special needs:

Resources

Rabbit Organisations

The Rabbit Charity
PO Box 23698
London N8 0WS
Tel. 020 8888 0001
Fax. 020 8888 8868
Info@bunny.org.uk
www.bunny.org.uk
The Rabbit Charity is an international charity for the welfare of rabbits (reg. No. 1068622). Members receive the quarterly magazine The Rabbit Habit® and details of the Bunny Hopline.

Bunny Buys
PO Box 23698
London N8 0WS
Tel. 020 8888 0001
Fax. 020 8888 8868
www.bunnybuys.com
shop@bunnybuys.com
The mail order company of The Rabbit Charity, sells everything from Busy Bunny Toys® and baskets to cable covers. All profits are donated to The Rabbit Charity.

House Rabbit Society
PO Box 1201
Alameda
CA 95401
USA
Tel. 510/521 4631
House Rabbit Society is a non-profit rescue and education organisation with chapters all over America. HRS publishes a quarterly newsletter and has lots of wonderful rescued bunnies available for adoption.

Rabbit Publications

The Rabbit Habit® is the quarterly magazine for members of The Rabbit Charity with articles on rabbit care, health, behaviour and house rabbits. For further details please contact The Rabbit Charity, PO Box 23698, London N8 0WS.

The Rabbit Charity also runs the Bunny Club for children. Members receive the quarterly newsletter The Carrot Gazette®. Details are available from The Bunny Club, PO Box 23698, London N8 0WS.

Rabbit Healthcare® is The Rabbit Charity's quarterly newsletter written by vets for vets. Details are available from The Rabbit Charity, PO Box 23698, London N8 0WS.

The House Rabbit Journal is the quarterly newsletter of the US House Rabbit Society. HRJ, PO Box 1201, Alameda, CA 94501, USA.

Note: The above publications are produced by charitable trusts and all profits are used to help rabbits in need. Additional donations help to rescue more rabbits.

Books

House Rabbit Handbook *by Marinell Harriman. Published by Drollery Press.*
The Really Useful Bunny Guide *by Carolina James. Published by TFH/Kingdom Books.*
Why does my rabbit? *by Anne McBride. Published by Souvenir Press.*
The Problem with Rabbits *by Pat Rees. Published by Greenfork.*